9/12

Salty Snacks

Salty Snacks

Make Your Own Chips, Crisps, Crackers,
Pretzels, Dips, and Other Savory Bites

Cynthia Nims

Photography by Jennifer Martiné

TEN SPEED PRESS
Berkeley

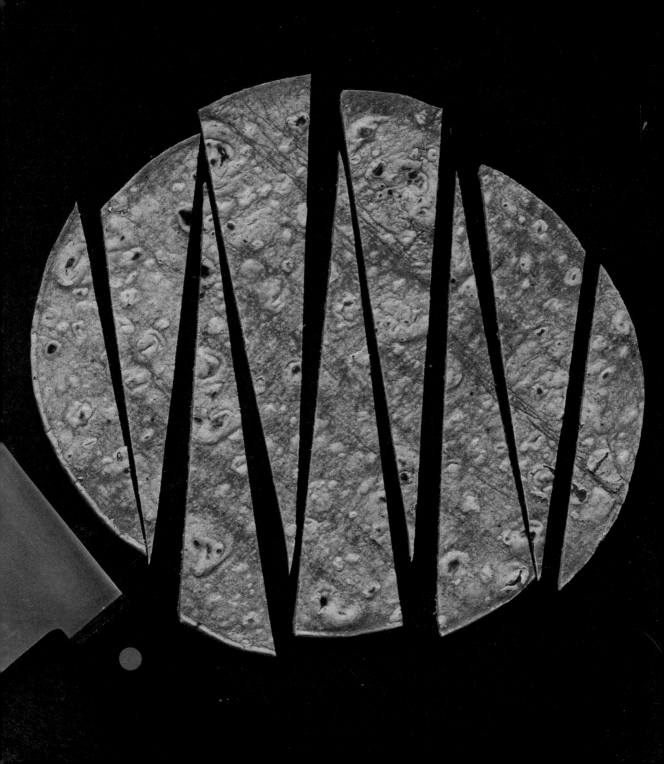

Contents

Acknowledgments

Many thanks to those who contributed their expertise, time, talents, and taste buds to the process of bringing this book together. For starters, I thank chef friends who helped me hone particular techniques, ideas, and recipes, including Kathy Casey, Matt Costello, Christina Orchid, Maxime Billet, Dana Tough, Marcia Sisley-Berger, and Adam Sappington. In the gluten-free department, friends Jeanne Sauvage and Shauna Ahern offered valuable input: many thanks! And I very much appreciate Barbara J. Pyper, MS, RD, offering me her ear to discuss nutritional aspects of snacks. When it came to gaining an industry perspective on the current state of interest in the world of salty snacks, Ron Tanner at the National Association for the Specialty Food Trade was most helpful.

I relish any chance to delve into the historical perspectives of a food or beverage subject. The context and frame of reference we gain by understanding the roots of what we're enjoying today makes the eating experience that much richer. A wide range of references, books, websites, even a History Channel hour devoted to the history of salty snacks all enhanced my appreciation of these foods. Two favorite references I turn to regularly for a bit of historic input on food are *The Oxford Companion to American Food and Drink* edited by Andrew F. Smith, and The Food Timeline at www.foodtimeline.org.

Special thanks to friend/neighbor/writer Susan Volland, who's always willing to jump in to help with a persnickety recipe, a bit of brainstorming, a critical editor's eye, and general encouragement.

Many thanks to my team of recipe testers: Michael Amend, Jeff Ashley, Mary Pyper, Barbara Nims, Ed Silver, Cathy Silvey, Dick Wood, Cathy Sander, and Tracey Wickersham. And thanks to the great many tasters who offered feedback and advice to help fine-tune the recipes over the months.

I'm thrilled to work with such a talented and enjoyable team of folks at Ten Speed Press. Cheers in particular to my editor, Lisa Westmoreland, who's got a keen eye for clarity and is a great collaborator. Thanks, too, to art director Betsy Stromberg, designer Colleen Cain, publicist Kara Van der Water, and publisher Aaron Wehner who oversees such a great crew. And to Jennifer Martiné, thanks for the luscious photos.

Finally, a big and loving thank you to my amazing husband, Bob, who is always willing to go with the flow of whatever project is in the works. Snacks again for dinner? "No problem," he said at each instance. Thanks, Love.

Cheers to you all.

Introduction

Without a doubt, salty-crunchy is my favorite food group. When declining another dessert or passing on the chocolate chip cookies, I've long explained it by saying that I have the opposite of a sweet tooth. A salty tooth, if there is such a thing. Any time salt and savory flavorings meet something that's crisp and snackable, I'm happy: tortilla chips, nuts, popcorn, crackers, and the most beloved of all, potato chips.

So I like to think of this book you're holding as something of a salt-lover's answer to all the cookie and sweet-treat cookbooks that come out each year. It is a book for everyone who has a salty tooth like me.

As a kid I'd not only snack on potato chips out of the bag but layer some between the peanut butter and jelly on a sandwich for a bit of salty-crunchy *je ne sais quoi*. It was love at first sight with that amazing invention Jiffy Pop, which enchanted by the sheer drama and magic it brought to the simple task of popping corn.

I even gravitated to what seems an unlikely snack for kids: smoked oysters. Nothing fancy, mind you, just those everyday flat tins of little smoky bivalves crammed into tight quarters. Crackers + smoked oysters = happy, even today. So, I was particularly charmed when attending a dinner in Seattle with New York City chef Gabrielle Hamilton while she was on tour with her book *Blood, Bones & Butter*. The first course included Triscuits topped with canned sardines and a dab of mustard. It's a standard on the bar menu at her restaurant, Prune, echoing memories of foods that sustained her in her earlier years.

So I know I'm not the only one with a personal, often nostalgic, attachment to salty treats. What I find interesting, though, is that when it comes to homemade snacks of the savory type, there are far fewer recipe resources at hand than there are for sweets. For whatever reason, we're not as accustomed to thinking of salty snacks as a made-from-scratch prospect. Among the first culinary adventures we have in the kitchen as kids is to press a cutter into a sheet of sugar cookie dough, or to stir the walnuts into a bowl of brownie batter. I don't know about you, but I never made rye crackers or savory puff pastry snacks with my mom when I was young. Why is that the case? It's time to stop relegating the task of cooking all our salty treats to commercial producers. Time to make some at home.

It's clear the American population has a taste for salty snacks. In a retail context, it is a bold and dynamic category to be sure. Just check out the chips/crackers/snack mix aisle at the grocery store. In most stores I visit, salty selections dwarf those for cookies and sweet snacks. Extensive research done by the National Association for the Specialty Food Trade in conjunction with Mintel International (a global market research firm) and SPINS (a company that analyzes the retail marketplace) shows dynamic growth in the sector. The resulting "State of the Specialty Food Industry" report cites that snack sales across all sectors, from specialty to mainstream, topped $11 billion in 2010, noting that figure as an 11 percent increase from 2008. As Ron Tanner, vice president of communications and education for NASFT, pointed out to me in January 2012, "Americans have always loved to snack. As people are getting more health conscious, they're looking to find new options." Companies are responding with an ever-increasing array of selections. He goes on to note that there are ingredients "you wouldn't think of—seaweed snacks, a lot of root vegetables, lots of international flavors—going into snacks these days." In November 2011, the *Supermarket News* website featured an article called "Whole Health: Different Chips," which cited some industry observers estimating that sales of salty snacks could hit $24 billion in a few years' time. That's a lot of popcorn and chips!

So, we love our salty snacks. We just don't make them at home all that often. My hope with this book is to inspire more playing around in the kitchen with salty-crunchy treats, the way we so easily gravitate to the kitchen to make a batch of cookies or some other sweet snack.

Modern Snack Evolution

Television and modern salty snacks grew up together in some ways. As the television set became the centerpiece of most American homes, food selections evolved to keep us from missing a moment of Arthur Godfrey and Hopalong Cassidy right there in our living rooms. After the TV dinners were finished and those folding metal TV trays tucked away, snack food made it easy to enjoy the show and not miss a beat. In the early 1950s, the Frito Kid was among the first snacky icons to charm TV viewers over the airwaves with the idea of a salty snack.

In *Betty Crocker's Picture Cookbook* released in 1950, a recipe for "Buttered or Cheese Kix" was among the first recipes that bridged breakfast cereal to snack food with little more than Kix tossed with melted butter (and grated Parmesan cheese, if you choose). You can take any vaguely puffy-crunchy cereal, embellish it with kindred ingredients such as pretzel sticks and nuts, toss with a seasoned butter, and bake until toasty. What's not to love? The cereal brand Chex released its namesake original Chex Mix recipe in the early 1950s; other similar snack blends went by the more general "TV snack mix" or "TV mix," or sometimes just "Party Mix." My snackable tribute to that legacy is on page 114.

Over the decades, salty snack selections have evolved demonstrably, from Chex Mix and Fritos to lentil chips and Peruvian potato chips. The diversity of prospects when it comes to salty-crunchy offerings helps fuel that growth: the endless potential chip flavorings (from spicy

Thai to malt vinegar), the different grains and flours that can be employed (chickpeas, green peas, black beans), the expansion to other chipable foods (sweet potatoes, taro, kale).

A big driver in recent salty developments is growing consumer interest in snacking without guilt and nibbling something tasty regardless of dietary restrictions or recommendations. Producers new and old, large and small are revisiting, refreshing, reinventing the realm of salty snacks and looking at them from every angle to suit every type of eater. It's why we see snack companies going all-natural with new products, forgoing lab-created flavoring and artificial coloring for natural flavorings and vegetable juices, touting whole grains, and even going gluten-free. You'll be ahead of the game when you're making these snacks from scratch at home. In your own kitchen, you've got control over the type and quality of ingredients you use. Whether the recipe you pick is retro-style or new-fangled, indulgent or wholesome, your reward is not only fresh and natural snacks but also snacks that are customized to suit your mood, your personality, and your palate.

Salty Snacks Defined

Merriam-Webster's Collegiate Dictionary, 11th edition, defines a snack as "food eaten between regular meals" and "food suitable for snacking." Just in case the reader isn't quite sure how to use snack in a sentence, they offer this example: "He had a snack of chips and dip." While I will always love a bag of potato chips and a bowl of onion dip, the world of possible snackage is much broader, more diverse, and more delicious than I think many realize. Interestingly, my 1941 edition of the *Webster New International Dictionary* makes little note of food relative to the primary meanings of the "snack" entry, instead relating the word as "to snatch something with the teeth" or "a snap, or bite, as of a dog." It takes until definition number four to get to "a slight, hasty repast." And that doesn't

well match the expectation of something delightful and satisfying when we reach for a snack today.

Generally I like to consider salty snacks as interlude food. They're there when we're feeling peckish between meals, when a real meal just isn't in the cards, or when we're on the go. They satisfy at any hour, from late-morning hunger pangs to midnight munchies.

Snacks should be convenient and unfussy. All of the recipes I present are essentially finger food, easy to serve from a bowl or platter, no utensils required, with minimal clean-up demanded of the cook. Snacking is generally done in small doses, a little nibble of something to accompany a cold drink or tide us over to dinner. Many recipes here lean toward bold tastes, so those small bites still serve up a fully satisfying level of flavor.

There are a few specific scenarios where salty snacks are naturally at home. One is certainly at the bar. Whether at a neighborhood brewpub, a fancy cocktail lounge, or the bar at your favorite restaurant, there's no denying that a cold beverage and something salty go hand in hand. Today bar menus tout a range of snacks to choose from, and some establishments may put out bowls of complimentary pistachios or pretzels to keep patrons happy, and thirsty. At the turn of the last century, in fact, there actually was a free lunch. Many saloons set out cheese, cured meats, maybe sardines, and sandwiches—all salty enough to encourage more imbibing!

There is an aperitif element to the savory snack as well, a civilized bridge that takes us from the workday toward dinner. I love how the French traditionally approach the aperitif hour; during the years I spent in France, I never tired of the ritual. One doesn't advance directly to the dinner table after the last chore of the day, or when stepping in the door from work. Instead it's into the living room, or even just mingling at the kitchen counter, to have a glass of wine, perhaps a kir. Out come the pistachios, chips, a dish of olives—small, very simple snacks to accompany the beverages and whet the appetite, no semblance of attempting to satisfy it. I've got Moroccan Spiced Olives (page 122), Stilton and Walnut Pinwheels (page 48), and Parsnip and Carrot Chips (page 23) as great options for the aperitif hour.

Convenience is a common factor of snacks as well. We often need them to be portable and sturdy, not requiring refrigeration or protection from getting smooshed in a backpack or briefcase. Some of the earliest such portable foods were more sustenance than snackage. Beef jerky and other dried meats developed out of necessity to prolong the protein benefit from a cow or bison. Jerky became one type of essential take-along food for trail-riders or any traveler who couldn't be otherwise assured of a source for his next meal. Over the decades it became a go-to convenience food; and in the past couple of years, it has been experiencing something of a resurgence on restaurant menus and among commercial snack offerings.

At The Country Cat restaurant in Portland, Oregon, chef-owner Adam Sappington makes beef jerky with a dose of celery salt among the seasonings, serving it as a garnish to the house Bloody Mary and as a very popular bar snack on the menu. That's a long and tasty trip from what used to be tucked into saddle bags out of necessity. Check out my recipe for Duck Jerky on page 102.

Salty snacks may comprise a gamut of petite treats, but if you add enough of those nibbles together, snacks can become a meal. Just consider the degree to which grazing is a beloved way of dining today. Serving an array of snacks at dinnertime is a fun shift away from the traditional big plate of meat/vegetable/starch to an evening meal composed of a number of small plates.

This certainly was the case while I was testing recipes. After a full day of cooking, my kitchen counter would be covered with various crackers, savory cookies, oven-roasted ingredients, maybe something pickled. I cherish having friends over to serve as guinea pigs and offer feedback, but I'd feel a bit uneasy about not having more than snacks to offer (in the back of my mind thinking, "Hey, we can always order a pizza if necessary . . ."). Without exception, folks loved the variety of things to nibble on and always assured me they left fully satisfied. I could tell they were having a lot of fun. It makes for a nice change of pace from the traditional dinner party.

Healthfulness and Snacks

Is it a bit daring to so boldly celebrate salt at the core of this project?

Salt is, after all, a white-hot-button topic in health news lately. And yet, it's an ingredient that provides our bodies with critical sodium, and one without which food would taste exponentially more bland. It's unlikely many of us are at risk for not consuming enough sodium each day, however. The problem lies in what is deemed to be a chronic overconsumption of salt by Americans today, most of which comes from processed and prepared foods (such as canned or convenience foods). Public health authorities, the medical community, and researchers weigh in frequently on the subject, and the Dietary Guidelines for Americans released in 2010 and the new MyPlate recommendations take a very conservative approach to sodium. But there's not universal consensus about the extent of health risks attributed to sodium and how much of the population is most at risk—everyone? Or just those in high-risk groups, such as people with high blood pressure or history of cardiovascular disease? It leaves us consumers with a cautious, or even fearful, relationship to an ingredient that's inextricably associated with good food. Based on a few different salty perspectives I've read, there's some consensus that of all the sources of sodium in our diets today, the salt we add ourselves to food—while cooking or on a plate we've been served—accounts for an average of just 10 percent or so of daily totals. Most important, that amount you add is up to you and you're aware of how much you've used, unlike with many prepared foods in which sodium levels can be sneaky. I don't fret much about the relatively small dose of salt I use when cooking and seasoning foods at home, but I do keep an eye on sodium levels in commercially prepared foods that might cross my path each day. For instance, one cup of the canned lentil soup I turn to for lunch some days could top 800 mg of sodium in one serving, while a handful of homemade crackers or a few of those Savory Hazelnut-Fig Shortbreads (page 77) will set me back just 150 mg or so.

I like to think about salt as a qualitative addition to our diets and the foods we enjoy. Sure, we might all do well to consume a bit less than we do. But using good salt in small doses where it really shines—boosting other flavors while cooking and adding a bit of texture to the eating experience—is to me a reasonable part of a diet that's healthier than one that relies heavily on commercially prepared foods.

By making these snacks at home, you have control over the amount of salt that ends up in the finished product. You can opt not to scatter

THE MAGIC OF PUFFY SNACKS

There is one category of snacks that I don't delve into with recipes in this book: the ever-delightful puffy snack. Tasty as they are, whether Asian shrimp chips or American cheese doodles, they're just not the easiest things to replicate at home—at least not without a penchant for more scientific elements of cooking and some extra attention to precision.

The concept behind what makes puffy snacks puffy isn't a complex one. It comes down to a combination of pressure, heat, and moisture. In fact, the process is echoed in the simple act of a kernel of popcorn popping. The kernel has a hard layer on the surface (the pericarp), with the perfect amount of residual water inside (thanks, Mother Nature!). When the kernel meets enough heat, that trapped water creates steam and expands, pressing up against the hull to create pressure, then—

poof—the surface gives way and the starchy center explodes into a puffy crunchy snack.

With a puffy snack such as shrimp crackers, known as *krupuk* in Indonesia or *bahn phong tom* in Vietnam, a batter is first made from shrimp paste, starch and/or flour, water, and seasonings. The batter is then steamed until set, cooled, thinly sliced, and dried. The slices replicate the corn kernel described earlier, in that the now-dry batter encloses tiny little pockets of residual water in each slice. When the slices hit a pan of hot fat, the trapped water boils, the steam expands, and it breaks through the hard surface to burst into a light, airy, puffy snack.

Pork rinds or "cracklins" are an all-natural puffy snack that follows the same principle as the shrimp crackers. (Note that some styles of rinds or cracklins are made by a simpler salt over the top of the crackers before baking, using poppy seeds or a favorite spice (such as cumin or a bit of cayenne) instead. If you've got health concerns that have you reducing salt in your diet, by all means make adjustments to the recipes to reflect that.

Many recipes in this book are naturally gluten-free. But I did also develop a few recipes specifically with gluten-free snackers in mind: Cumin Lentil Crackers (page 74), Almond–Olive Oil Crackers (page 68), and Seedy Cornmeal Bread Sticks (page 60). There are also a couple of recipes that use nonwheat flours: Crisp Shrimp with Shichimi Togarashi (page 90) and Onion Pakoras with Cilantro Sauce (page 139). If you'll be sharing these snacks with someone who has celiac disease or any condition that results in extreme reactions to consumption of gluten, it's important to verify that all the ingredients you're using are gluten-free; look for specific designation on the package or check with the manufacturer. Some ingredients, such as baking powder, may have additives that contain gluten. Cornmeal, oats, and buckwheat may have been processed in a facility that also processes

method that leaves them very crisp but hardly puffy; I'm speaking here of specifically the light and puffy version.) Pieces of pork skin and/or fat are cooked (generally by a moist method, such as simmering or pressure-cooking), cooled, and dried as for the shrimp crackers. If the residual moisture's just right and the amount of fat is in good balance, the dried skin will puff up dramatically into a light snack when it hits hot oil. When Spur restaurant opened in Seattle, chefs Dana Tough and Brian McCracken garnished a mussel recipe with classic pork cracklins made in that traditional fashion. But they found, even making them as often as they did, that they were finicky to produce in a consistent manner. The properties of the dried skin needed to be exactly right to puff properly. So they went about developing a new kind of pork cracklin that is created rather like those shrimp crackers. They start with a richly flavored ham broth,

blend it with tapioca flour, then steam the dough to solidify it before slicing, dehydrating, and frying. These cracklins are so popular that they now stand alone as a beloved appetizer on the menu at their new restaurant, The Coterie Room, served with a decadent dip of melted cheese with truffle.

In the world of the American-style cheesy puff snack, the baseline science is the same, even if the process is a bit different (and not exactly the same for all manufacturers). The starting point is typically a dough based on cornmeal, which is forced through an extruder at very high pressure. When the pressurized dough passes through the die opening of the extruder, the change in pressure causes it to expand significantly. The puffs are then usually baked (sometimes fried) to remove excess moisture and set the form. Finally, the light and puffy bites are tossed with cheesy flavorings.

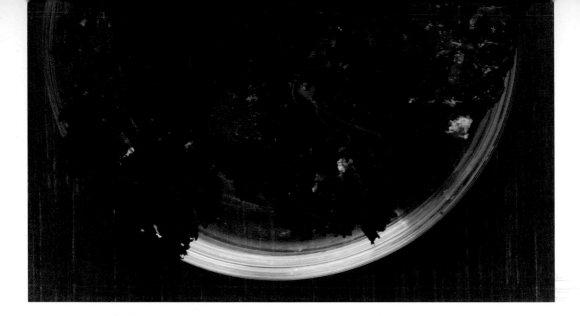

wheat. Be sure to check the label whenever avoiding gluten is critical.

I trust that those already cooking and eating gluten-free know the ropes in terms of where they'll need to make adjustments to recipes, perhaps employing a favorite gluten-free flour mix in place of all-purpose flour. For others, you'll have some hints in these pages of dishes you can make for that next neighborhood potluck or when gluten-free friends come over for dinner.

About the Recipes

When it comes to portion sizes for these recipes, much is relative. After all, for a party at which there are a number of other noshes, a dozen folks can nibble at a bowl of the Popcorn with Chili-Lime Butter and Cotija (page 112). But when settling in for your seventeenth viewing of *Rear Window,* you and a pal can go through the whole bowl yourself. When determining yields for the recipes, I ended up shooting for some average between the extremes on servings.

Also, when cutting crackers, there's an endless possibility to the shapes and sizes that can be cut: little squares, long slender strips, big triangles—heck, even butterflies and cowboy hats if you want. I offer ballpark yields on the crackers based on the shape I spell out in the recipe, but by all means follow your own muse and shape the crackers as you'd like. Your yield may vary accordingly.

Recipes all have a stand-alone quality, autonomous in their snackability, worthy of eating solo as an afternoon bite or nibbling with a cocktail before dinner. Some might also make a great partner for a bowl of soup or salad, or be ideal cheese-tray accompaniments, or have some other spin-off potential that will be noted in the recipes.

I offer some specific sauces and dips for a handful of the recipes where there is a particularly keen match to be made (such as dill sauce for the fried cornichons on page 140). Otherwise you'll find other dips and spreads in the final chapter that will be versatile partners for many of the snack recipes you find here.

When it comes to time commitment, the recipes in this collection range from the lickety-split to the more involved recipes you might save for weekend cooking. You'll have plenty to turn to when time is of the essence—Salami Chips with Grainy Mustard Dip (page 104), Crostini with Pine Nuts and Mint Ricotta (page 41), and Coconut Crisps with Basil and Chiles (page 28) are a few tasty examples. When you have a little more time on your hands, you might want to try the Taralli (page 78), Duck Jerky (page 102), or Olive Focaccia with Lemon (page 52). But really, there's not much here that's super elaborate. There are a great many recipes in this book that will have you snacking on something to satisfy your salty tooth in about the time it takes to whip up a batch of cookies!

Tools and Techniques

Here are some notes about favorite tools, tips, and techniques I use in this book. They're intended to help you make the most of your salty snack creations, often by making the process easier, quicker, and more consistent.

BAKING SHEETS

You'll see that I consistently call for "rimmed baking sheets" for the savory cookies, crackers, and other baked goods in the book. In some cases, it's a distinctly practical matter because whatever's being baked will likely drip or ooze in the process. Other times it's more for insurance. When I have baked on a purely flat sheet, I've found it doesn't take much to knock the pan just right and have your treats slip off the edge. So, in the long run, I just go "rimmed" without fail. And this is one kitchen product I love to stock up on at the restaurant supply store. There are lots of lovely sizes and types of baking sheets you can find in traditional cookware stores, but the type you'll find in restaurant supply stores are sturdy, durable, long lasting, simple, and inexpensive. What's known as the "half sheet pan" is an ideal all-purpose size for home use: 18 by 13 inches.

DOUGH DOCKER

For many of the cracker recipes, it's a good idea to pierce the surface of the dough pretty well to avoid puffed-up air pockets forming during baking. "Docking" the dough before baking helps alleviate that problem. A tool used by professional bakers, called a dough docker, is a rolling pin–like cylinder with little spikes sticking out of it. Rolled over the surface of the dough, it quickly and evenly pierces the dough. I, however, tend to still just reach for an old-school fork when docking is needed. The denser the dough, the less problematic puffing may be, so not all cracker recipes necessarily need docking. But it's a good idea for most of them.

GRINDING

For a few different recipes in this book, I turn to my trusty multipurpose grinder. Whether it's for seeds (like the sesame seeds for the pan-fried chiles on page 136), spices (pink peppercorns for the crisps on page 36), or dried foods, such as mushrooms (for the Porcini Choux Puffs, page 49), I rely on one go-to tool: a recommissioned blade-type coffee grinder that is now delegated solely to kitchen chores such as this. Inexpensive, easy to use, and easy to clean—three of my favorite things.

BAKING SHEET LINERS

It's become a habit that most every time I reach for one of my baking sheets I also reach for a piece of parchment paper, a baking mat, or a sheet of foil to line the pan. Sometimes it's a matter of necessity to help ensure that the item being baked doesn't stick. But other times, to be perfectly honest, I do so out of laziness (I prefer to think of it as efficiency). Fatty, sticky, cheesy items can leave behind quite a mess on the surface of the pan. It's so much easier to clean up by lifting out the silicone mat or crumpling up the parchment paper. It saves soaking, scrubbing, and scraping the baking sheet to clean it, and I figure it does the pan a favor as well.

MANDOLINE SLICER

I know some folks out there have steady, surgeon-like knife skills that make cutting very thin slices, as for the apple slices on page 27, no problem at all. That's not me. And for a recipe such as that one, there are technical reasons to take extra care in slicing. A tool like a mandoline helps assure each slice is even in its thickness, and from slice to slice you're likely to have more consistency in thicknesses. I'm rarely much of a stickler for such things, but here that consistency translates to even cooking and a little more control over the final results.

Not all mandolines have the same range and flexibility of thickness options; some offer a handful of settings to choose from, others have a screw-type adjustment that allows you more control over thickness. I actually have two types of mandolines, one small handheld mandoline with a porcelain blade that I love for lots of everyday uses—such as slicing radishes for a salad. My Japanese-style mandoline is a bit bigger, with a versatile screw adjustment, and a few different julienne attachments to tackle different types of slicing needs. Oh, and please don't be like me. Always use the hand-guard or one of those nifty cut-protection gloves. Though I'm trying to get better about that . . .

MINI FOOD PROCESSOR

It wasn't something that had been on my wish list for the kitchen, but after being given a mini food processor, it became a reliable pal any time that I have just a small batch of something to finely chop or puree. The type I use is a stand-alone baby version of a regular food processor. Many newer full-size food processors come with smaller bowl inserts, which I'm sure work great as well. I still use my full-size processor quite a lot; but when it's just a cup or so of something that needs attention, the larger processor is less effective, and I'm glad to have the mini version.

OILS

The everyday oil I use for most stove top cooking is basic "pure" olive oil. It's kept in a pretty bottle alongside the stove, ready to drizzle into a skillet or saucepan at a moment's notice. Really, it's a good all-purpose oil that I also use in vinaigrette dressings, to rub over a chicken before roasting, and for other common uses. I do have some lovely extra-virgin olive oil in the cupboard at all times, too, to use for a more robust style of vinaigrette, to drizzle over braised kale just before serving, and other occasions when the richer, more flavorful oil is preferable. In many of these recipes, when the oil is coating an ingredient or contributing a touch of richness to a dough, any good olive oil will do. Often, a vegetable oil will be fine, too, but I tend to turn to olive oil for the added depth of flavor.

When it comes to deep frying, it's time to reach for the more neutrally flavored oils. I often use canola in these cases, or soybean oil (which I've seen labeled as generic "vegetable oil").

HEATING OIL

The recipes in this book that involve deep-frying call for slightly varying oil temperatures, depending on the shape, thickness, density, and other characteristics of the foods being cooked.

To achieve and maintain whatever temperature you need requires just a bit more attention than simply setting your stove to medium heat and leaving it there. Different styles and generations of stoves inherently heat differently to begin with, and calibrating your stove setting to maintain an exact 350°F could be a challenge.

Instead, I suggest you heat the oil over medium heat until the intended temperature is reached, using an instant-read thermometer to verify the temperature. Then add the food and cook as noted in the recipe. Once the food's been added, the oil temperature will drop a bit, which is perfectly natural. Check the oil temperature after that batch of food has been removed; you'll likely need to give it a minute or two of reheating time to achieve the desired temperature again before adding the next batch. If you find the oil either heats too quickly (surpassing the desired temperature), or too slowly, adjust the heat under the pan as needed. Avoid frying over medium-high heat if at all possible; I prefer medium to avoid overheating the oil.

PASTA MACHINE

It may seem odd to be reaching for the pasta machine for making snacks. But this is a trick I first learned from friend and amazing chef Christina Orchid, when sitting in her kitchen nibbling on crackers she'd made that afternoon. A pasta machine makes quick work of rolling out dough for crackers. Not only does it make the rolling out faster, it also helps create crackers of even thickness that will bake more consistently.

I find it easier to work with smaller portions of dough in the pasta machine than when rolling by hand. The more dough you start with, the longer the final sheet of thin dough will be, which can become awkward to handle through the rollers. Many of these recipes call for cutting the dough into four portions for rolling out, so you might start with eight portions if using the pasta machine, at least until you get the hang of it.

Start by flattening a portion of dough with your fingers first, then feed it through the thickest roller setting once or twice (sprinkle a tiny bit of flour on the dough if needed). Then set the dough horizontally on the counter and fold in the rounded ends toward the center—the packet should measure about $3^1/2$ inches across. With those folded edges now the left and right sides, feed the dough back through the thickest rollers one more time. This helps create a more rectangular shape.

Reduce the roller setting by one level of thickness and pass the dough through again. Continue reducing the rollers one setting at a time (dusting lightly with flour as needed) until you've rolled the dough to a thickness of about $1/16$ inch. On my classic hand-crank pasta machine, that's about setting number 5; on your pasta machine that may be a different setting level. I find most crackers to be ideal at this thickness; I have gone to setting number 6 at times for a slightly thinner, more delicate cracker, but be sure to watch the baking carefully—they'll brown more quickly at that thickness.

After rolling out the crackers, I usually just wipe down the machine with a dry or lightly dampened paper towel to clean it. If the dough has butter in it, you may find there's some buttery residue on the underside of the roller area; be sure to wipe that clean before putting the machine away.

PASTRY CUTTERS

For most of the cracker recipes here, I call for using a pizza cutter or pastry wheel to form the individual crackers. I much prefer this to using a knife blade for this particular task. Even the sharpest knife can stretch the dough as it draws across it, and you also are at less risk of marring the work surface below. The rolling blades of the pizza cutter or pastry wheel glide more effortlessly across the dough. And some pastry cutters have a fluted rather than straight edge, so you can add a little panache to the presentation. In fact, one pastry cutter I have includes both a plain and fluted wheel, so I can go either route on a whim.

ROASTING CHILES OR PEPPERS

Roasting whole fresh chiles or peppers before using them accomplishes a few different things: the flesh becomes tender, the flavor mellows a bit, and the skin becomes much easier to remove. The process can either be done stovetop or in the oven. Set the whole chiles or peppers over a gas flame on the stove, or in a shallow pan under the broiler, until the skin blackens, turning occasionally to roast evenly, 10 to 15 minutes total. Put the chiles or peppers in a plastic bag, securely seal it, and set aside to cool. When cool, peel away and discard the skin. Remove the core and seeds and dice, slice, or otherwise prepare the chiles or peppers as needed.

SPRINKLING SEASONINGS

It can be hard to do an even job of sprinkling a spice over a broad surface, as with the chile powder that seasons tortillas on page 34. But we can take a hint from bakers who dust powdered sugar over cakes by using a sieve. For finely ground spices, a fine sieve is best. Gently spoon the powdered spice into the sieve and hold it a few inches above the surface of whatever you're seasoning, tapping from the side of the sieve so that a light dusting of the spice falls below. A medium-grid sieve will be better for coarser seasonings, such as flavored salts. For combinations such as citrus zest and salt, I sometimes take them for a spin in my spice grinder or mini food processor to create a

SALT NOTES

Technically, all salts are created equal. Whether it's a lovely pink flake salt from the Murray River in Australia or a standard everyday table salt, the sodium they serve up gram for gram is the same core mineral: sodium chloride. The way in which salts may differ in a dietary context is the other beneficial minerals they might also contain.

But teaspoon for teaspoon, salts are not all the same, an important consideration when cooking. A fine salt, whether traditional table salt or artisanal sea salt, more densely fills a teaspoon. When measuring fine salt you'll get about 6 grams per teaspoon, of which roughly 2200 milligrams is sodium. But a teaspoon of a flaky or coarse salt, such as kosher, fills the spoon more loosely and will weigh more like 3 grams, with about 1100 milligrams of sodium. (Those values are based on salt products I have on my kitchen counter, exact weights can vary.) Using a teaspoon measure of fine salt when kosher salt is called for would surely leave you with overly salty results.

For most of the recipes in my previous books, salt has been used by the pinch or to taste. But with the salty focus of this cookbook, more detail was needed. I tested all of these recipes with kosher salt. You can use other moderately coarse or flaky salts—such as fleur de sel—in place of the kosher salt at equal measures. If, however, you're using a fine salt, I recommend you use half the amount called for in the recipes.

finer texture that then falls more easily through the mesh of the sieve for even sprinkling. But I often just pick up pinches of seasoned salt with my fingers and sprinkle by hand.

Kitchen Safety

Some of the recipes in this book include raw eggs or raw seafood. When these foods are consumed raw, there is always the risk that bacteria (which is killed by proper cooking) may be present. For this reason, when serving these foods raw, always buy the freshest eggs and seafood that are available from a reliable source, storing them in the refrigerator until they are served. Because of the health risks associated with the consumption of bacteria that can be present in raw eggs and raw seafood, these foods should not be consumed by infants, small children, pregnant women, the elderly, or anyone with a compromised immune system.

SALTY HOLIDAYS

Many of those quirky food-related national "holidays" we hear about now and then are relegated to sweets—September 19 is National Butterscotch Pudding Day, February 28 is National Chocolate Soufflé Day, June 12 is National Peanut Butter Cookie Day, among many dozens more. But some salty treats make it on the culinary calendar as well. Should you need one more excuse to indulge in your favorite salty nibble, consider adding these to your datebook.

February 24: National Tortilla Chip Day

March 5: National Cheese Doodle Day

March 14: National Potato Chip Day

March 23: National Chips & Dip Day and National Melba Toast Day

April 26: National Pretzel Day

And the whole month of February is deemed a celebration of National Snack Food Month. Probably due to all those dark winter hours spent in front of the television, between the Super Bowl and television "sweeps." When the next February rolls around, you can celebrate with plenty of new snack ideas in these pages!

Chips and Crisps

Let's get right to the heart of the matter with some of the most salty-crunchy treats around—leading with the most quintessential of them all, the beloved potato chip. This chapter includes a range of items that are toasted, baked, or lightly fried to a delicate, flavorful crunch. From wonton skins to fresh kale, from slivers of coconut to thinly sliced apple, the diversity of this arena of snack potential may surprise you.

Potato Chips with Herbed Clam Dip | 18

Duck Fat Potato Chips | 20

Kabocha Squash Chips | 21

Parsnip and Carrot Chips | 23

Kale Chips with Lemon and Ginger | 24

Portabella Chips | 26

Sichuan Pepper Apple Chips | 27

Coconut Crisps with Basil and Chiles | 28

Aleppo Pepper Phyllo Crisps | 30

Soy-Wasabi Wonton Crisps | 32

Pita Chips with Hazelnut and Parmesan | 33

Spicy Tortilla Crisps with Queso Fundido | 34

Parmesan–Pink Peppercorn Crisps | 36

Anchovy Crisps | 37

Potato Chips *with Herbed Clam Dip*

This is the quintessential salty snack, if you ask me. The potato chip has that ideal balance of crunch and salty goodness that makes for perfect snacking. For the clam dip, lemony herbs—such as lemon verbena and lemon thyme—are great choices to add to the mix, along with whatever else is at hand (or perhaps in your herb garden). | **Makes 6 to 8 servings**

Herbed Clam Dip

- 2 (6^1/$_2$-ounce) cans minced clams, well drained
- ^{1}/$_2$ cup sour cream
- ^{1}/$_4$ cup top-quality mayonnaise
- ^{1}/$_4$ cup plain yogurt (preferably whole or low-fat)
- 3 tablespoons minced green onion, white and pale green portions
- 4 tablespoons mixed chopped fresh herbs (flat-leaf parsley, chives, tarragon, basil, lemon thyme, lemon verbena, and/or bronze fennel)
- 1 teaspoon white wine vinegar
- ^{1}/$_2$ teaspoon kosher salt or flaky or coarse sea salt

  Pinch cayenne pepper

  Vegetable oil, for frying
- 2 large russet potatoes (about 1^1/$_2$ pounds), scrubbed and well dried

  Kosher salt or flaky or coarse sea salt, for sprinkling

To make the dip, combine the clams, sour cream, mayonnaise, yogurt, green onions, 3 tablespoons of the herbs, vinegar, salt, and cayenne in a medium bowl and stir well to mix. Cover and refrigerate for at least 2 hours to allow the flavors to meld. The dip can be made up to 2 days in advance.

To make the potato chips, pour about 2 inches of oil into a large heavy saucepan (the oil should not come more than halfway up the sides of the pan). Bring to 350°F over medium heat.

Trim about ^{1}/$_2$ inch from the end of a potato and use a mandoline (see page 10) to cut about half of the potato into thin slices (about ^{1}/$_{16}$ inch thick). Lay the slices on a paper towel and top the potatoes with another paper towel, patting to dry a bit.

When the oil is hot, gently add 10 to 12 of the potato slices and fry until crisp and medium brown, about 3 minutes, stirring gently now and then to ensure the slices aren't sticking together. Lift out the slices with a slotted spoon and drain on paper towels, sprinkling right away with a bit of the salt. Continue frying the rest of the potatoes in the same fashion, slicing more when needed and allowing the oil to reheat between batches as needed. (Slicing the potatoes just before they are fried helps avoid discoloration.)

When all the potatoes have been fried, transfer them to a bowl and sprinkle the remaining 1 tablespoon chopped herbs over them. Serve right away, with the dip alongside.

POTATO CHIP HISTORY

It's hard to know for sure when the first thin slice of potato met a pan of hot fat. I imagine it predates 1853, though that's the year the potato chip had its most public and storied debut. One Mr. George Crum is deemed the inventor of the snack that has gone on to make millions of nibblers so happy. As chef at Moon's Lake House in Saratoga Springs, New York, he was apparently unhappy when a customer sent back an order of French fries claiming they were too thick. He's said to have reacted with a "so, you want thin French fries, do you?" attitude and cooked up a new batch of super-thin "fries"—and the potato chip was born, originally dubbed the "Saratoga chip."

Interestingly, the crisp treat we now associate with snacking remained in the purview of restaurant offerings for a few decades, something to accompany a steak or pork chop, eaten while sitting properly at the table. It wasn't until the late 1800s that potato chips first showed up in retail channels. Clevelander William Tappenden started distributing chips made on a small scale in his own home. He then went on to build the first full-scale potato chip factory in 1895 as their popularity boomed.

A couple points of historical record gave potato chips a major boost, not only in sales but in securing their place as an indelible part of the country's food culture. One was the repeal of Prohibition, when there were lots of thirsty people in the United States, and they all needed something to snack on while they sipped their favorite drinks out in the open. With potato chips on hand, often at just a nickel a bag, the 1930s saw a nice little bump in devotion to the snack.

During World War II, many commodities were rationed in order to reserve resources for the war effort. Rationing hit America's kitchens in some beloved categories, such as butter, sugar, coffee, and cheese. But salt was not rationed, and potatoes were in good supply. So despite many hardships during the war years, potato chips were around to provide some comfort in the form of an increasingly beloved salty treat.

Duck Fat Potato Chips

Okay, sure, this is total decadence. But we deserve that now and again, right? All things in moderation? You can sometimes find ready-to-use rendered duck fat in well-stocked meat counters or butcher shops and from online sources. Or, if you've made the Five-Spice Duck Skin (page 101), then you've got the perfect little stash of duck fat. That lingering essence of five-spice powder from the duck skin recipe will only make these chips more delicious. | **Makes 4 servings**

About 1 cup (8 ounces) duck fat

8 ounces small Yukon Gold potatoes, scrubbed and well dried

1/2 teaspoon kosher salt or flaky or coarse sea salt

Put the duck fat in a medium heavy saucepan and heat over medium heat. The fat will not be very deep, so it can be difficult to measure temperature at that level, but about 350°F will be ideal. The duck fat may smoke slightly; if it smokes more than a little, reduce the heat under the pan. While the fat is heating, use a mandoline (see page 10) to thinly slice one of the potatoes (about 1/16 inch thick). To test the heat of the fat, add 1 slice of the potato; it should bubble actively but not brown quickly.

Add 10 to 12 of the potato slices and fry until lightly and evenly browned, 1 to 2 minutes, gently stirring occasionally with a slotted spoon to ensure the slices aren't sticking together. Lift them out with the slotted spoon and scatter on paper towels to drain, sprinkling them lightly with salt. Continue slicing and cooking the remaining potatoes in batches. (Slicing the potatoes just before they'll be fried helps avoid discoloration.)

Transfer the potato chips to a serving bowl and serve right away. The chips will be best served shortly after frying.

Kabocha Squash Chips

Kabocha squash has a nice starchy, firm flesh that takes well to this preparation. You don't even need to skin the squash first; in slices this thin, the flavor of the skin melds nicely with the sweeter flesh. The squash maintains a sweet nutty flavor even as it darkens to medium brown in color, unlike some vegetables that turn a bit bitter as the color darkens. | **Makes 4 to 6 servings**

$1/2$ small (2- to $2^1/2$-pound) kabocha squash, seeds scooped out and discarded

1 tablespoon olive oil

$1/2$ teaspoon kosher salt or flaky or coarse sea salt

Pinch of freshly ground black pepper

Preheat the oven to 325°F. Line 2 rimmed baking sheets with parchment paper or silicone baking mats and set 2 oven racks at the centermost positions.

Use a mandoline (see page 10) to slice the squash into $1/16$-inch slices and put them in a large bowl. Toss them with the oil to evenly coat, then arrange them in a single layer on the baking sheets; the slices can be snug but avoid touching as much as possible. Season the squash lightly with the salt and pepper.

Bake until lightly browned, no longer pliable, and mostly crisp (they'll continue to crisp a bit as they cool), about 30 minutes, switching the pans two or three times for even baking. Some slices may be done before others; use a metal spatula to transfer them to a wire rack to cool while you continue baking the rest.

Let cool completely, then put the chips in a bowl for serving. The chips will be best the day they are baked.

BAKED VEGETABLE CHIPS

I played around with a lot of different types of baked vegetable chips in an effort to come up with some alternatives to the delectable and beloved fried potato chip (of which I have two options in this collection, on pages 18 and 20). I found a number of my test subjects to be just a bit too persnickety to ensure reliable, consistent results. This was particularly true of turnips and beets with their natural sugars that make them prone to burning, so they went from flabby and soft (though delicious) to hard and burnt in unpredictable fashion. Kabocha squash (here) and portabella mushrooms (page 26) are a couple vegetables, however, that did work well, producing delightful results.

Parsnip *and* Carrot Chips

Choose the largest and broadest carrots and parsnips among those available at the store; smaller, more slender ones won't form large enough strips to be fruitful for frying. These have a light and delicate crunch and natural sweetness that make for an interesting change of pace from the traditional potato chip. | **Makes 4 to 6 servings**

---

3 large carrots (about 1 pound)

2 large parsnips (about 1 pound)

Vegetable oil, for frying

1 teaspoon kosher salt or flaky or coarse sea salt

¹/₂ teaspoon minced fresh thyme

After peeling one of the carrots, use the vegetable peeler to peel away long strips from the whole length of the carrot, allowing the strips to drop into a large bowl. Turn the carrot in your hand about one-quarter turn after every 4 or 5 strips, so you'll generally have strips of similar width and length overall. Do the same with the remaining carrots and the parsnips, both of which have a tough core that should be discarded once you get there (the color tends to change slightly).

Pour about 2 inches of oil into a large heavy saucepan (the oil should not come more than halfway up the sides of the pan). Bring to 375°F over medium heat.

While the oil is heating, combine the salt and thyme in a small dish and rub them together between your fingers for a bit to release the aromatics of the thyme.

Carefully add a handful of the vegetable strips to the oil and fry until lightly browned and crisp, 1 to 2 minutes. Use the back of a slotted spoon to gently press the strips down into the oil and spread them out a bit to help ensure even cooking. When crisped, lift out the strips and scatter them on paper towels to drain. Repeat with the remaining vegetable strips, allowing the oil to reheat between batches as needed.

Transfer the chips to a serving bowl, sprinkle the thyme-salt mixture over them, and serve. They will be best served shortly after frying.

Kale Chips *with Lemon and Ginger*

These might taste a bit indulgent, but in fact this is one salty-crunchy snack that's quite healthy. You can reduce the amount of olive oil to a mere misting from a sprayer if you prefer, and certainly you can use less salt to make this snack even healthier. Regular kale is rather curly relative to flatter lacinato/dinosaur kale; it takes a few extra moments to evenly coat the leaves with the olive oil. Results are equally delicious using either type of kale.

The kale takes on a bit of a bitter flavor even when lightly browned, so be sure to keep an eye on things toward the end of cooking and pull the leaves when they're dry and rigid but still deep green.

I've tried this with ground coriander seed in place of the grated fresh ginger, and that's pretty tasty, too! | **Makes 4 to 6 servings**

---

1 bunch (about 7 ounces) kale, rinsed and well dried

1 tablespoon olive oil, plus more if needed

1 teaspoon finely grated lemon zest

1 teaspoon finely grated fresh ginger

3/4 teaspoon kosher salt or flaky or coarse sea salt

Preheat the oven to 300°F. Line 2 baking sheets with parchment paper or silicone baking mats. Set 2 oven racks at the centermost positions.

Trim the tough stems from the kale leaves. Cut larger leaves crosswise into 3- to 4-inch portions; smaller leaves can be baked as is. Put the kale in a large bowl, drizzle 1 tablespoon of the olive oil over the leaves, and toss well with your hands to evenly coat the leaves with oil. The curlier them, the more you'll want to use your fingers to rub a bit of oil into the nooks and crannies. Just a light gloss of oil is the goal; drizzle another teaspoon or two over if needed,

but avoid excessive oil. Arrange the kale pieces on the prepared baking sheets, the leaves touching each other as little as possible.

Combine the lemon zest, ginger, and salt in a small bowl and use your fingers to rub the ingredients together well. (Be sure to do this at the last minute.) Sprinkle the salt mixture over the kale leaves.

Bake for 10 minutes. Switch the baking sheets and continue baking until the leaves are dry and rigid but not browned, 10 to 12 minutes longer. If some leaves at the outer edges of the baking sheets are ready earlier, transfer them to a wire rack and continue baking the remaining leaves for a few minutes.

Use a metal spatula to transfer the leaves to a wire rack to cool. Serve on a platter or in a broad shallow bowl. The kale chips are best on the day they are made but can be stored for up to 1 day in an airtight container.

Portabella Chips

This was inspired by a visit to the Pacific Northwest Mushroom Festival where I'd done a cooking demonstration. While there I tasted a snack-style dried shiitake mushroom that was pretty amazing, simple as could be, seasoned only with salt and pepper, but with deep flavor that went beyond what you'd expect from a mushroom. I've used dried mushrooms as an ingredient many times and knew the concentrated flavor they take on when dried. But I'd never really thought of mushrooms as snack material before.

Large portabella mushrooms are easier to work with than the shiitakes I also experimented with. I was surprised by the element of cocoa flavor that the mushroom slices took on after their spell in the oven. Nothing more than salt and pepper is needed, not even a smidge of oil.

| Makes 4 to 6 servings

---

2 portabella mushrooms, stems discarded or saved for another use, caps cut into $1/8$-inch slices

$1/2$ teaspoon kosher salt or flaky or coarse sea salt

Pinch of freshly ground black pepper

Preheat the oven to 250°F. Line 2 rimmed baking sheets with parchment paper or silicone baking mats. Set 2 oven racks at the centermost positions.

Arrange the mushroom slices on the baking sheets; the slices can be snug but avoid touching as much as possible. Sprinkle the mushrooms lightly with the salt and pepper.

Bake until well dried and no longer pliable, about $1^1/4$ hours, switching the pans after 30 minutes and turning the slices over after 45 minutes. Some slices may be done before others, so use a metal spatula to transfer them to a wire rack to cool while the rest continue drying.

Let cool completely before serving. The portabella chips will be best the same day they were dried, but any extra will keep for up to 1 day in an airtight container.

Sichuan Pepper Apple Chips

If you have three baking sheets and three oven racks, there will be enough apple slices to do a triple load; otherwise, you may want to dry just one apple at a time. Or, if you have a dehydrator tucked away in your household somewhere, this would be a great time to use it, following manufacturer's instructions.

You can core the whole apples before you slice them if you like, but the small fibrous bits at the center become crisp along the way and aren't unpleasant if left in the slices. Just flick out the seeds as you go. | **Makes 4 to 6 servings**

---

1 teaspoon Sichuan peppercorns

1 teaspoon kosher salt or flaky or coarse sea salt

2 firm, crisp apples, such as Fuji or Braeburn

Preheat the oven to 200°F. Line 3 baking sheets with parchment paper or silicone baking mats. Set 3 oven racks at the centermost positions.

Using a spice or coffee grinder (see page 10) or a mortar and pestle, finely grind the Sichuan peppercorns. Add the salt and grind a few moments longer to blend the salt and pepper. Transfer the mixture to a small bowl.

Peel the apples, coring them whole if you wish. Use a mandoline (see page 10) to cut the apples across into very thin slices (about $1/16$ inch thick). Remove the seeds from the slices.

Arrange the apple slices on the prepared baking sheets; they can be snug but should not touch. Lightly sprinkle the Sichuan pepper/salt mixture over the apple slices.

Bake until just lightly browned and quite dry, about $1^1/2$ hours, switching the pans every 30 minutes for even cooking. Transfer the apple slices to a wire rack to cool and crisp.

The apple chips will be best on the day they are baked.

Coconut Crisps *with Basil and Chiles*

I've learned to add extra shredded coconut to the pan when I'm toasting it for a recipe, since I can't keep myself from nibbling. This recipe touts the inherent snackability of toasted coconut, with added panache from fresh basil and serrano chile. If you're comfortable tackling a whole coconut, see the box for tips. Otherwise I love the simplicity of coconut "chips," broad flat shavings available from health food stores, specialty shops, or online sources (see page 154). | **Makes 6 to 8 servings**

---

3 cups (about 6 ounces) unsweetened coconut chips

2 tablespoons unsalted butter, melted

3 tablespoons minced fresh basil

2 teaspoons minced serrano chile

1 teaspoon kosher salt or flaky or coarse sea salt

Preheat the oven to 325°F. Line a rimmed baking sheet with parchment paper or a silicone baking mat.

Put the coconut in a medium bowl and drizzle the melted butter over, tossing gently to evenly coat the shavings without breaking up the coconut chips. Sprinkle the basil, chile, and salt over and toss well to evenly coat the coconut. Scatter the coconut on the prepared baking sheet. Bake until lightly browned and aromatic, stirring occasionally, about 12 minutes. Keep a close eye on the progress; the coconut can go from lightly browned to burned and bitter very quickly. You may want to stir more often nearer the end of the cooking time. Take the coconut from the oven and let cool on the baking sheet.

Transfer the coconut to a serving bowl, or store in an airtight container for up to 2 days.

FRESH COCONUT CHIPS

If you want to make fresh coconut chips yourself, begin by preheating the oven to 350°F. Carefully pierce the eyes of a whole brown coconut with an ice pick or other sturdy slender tool. Pour out the coconut water. Bake the coconut until the shell cracks a bit, 15 to 20 minutes. Set aside to cool. Reduce the oven temperature to 200°F.

Use a hammer or mallet to crack the coconut in half. With the tip of a small sharp knife, score the coconut meat down the center of each half. Working carefully, slip the tip of the knife between the meat and the shell, twisting the blade of the knife slowly and steadily to separate the meat from the shell in the largest pieces you can.

With a vegetable peeler, cut long, thin shavings from the longest edges of the coconut pieces, working over a bowl to capture the shavings as they fall. Shavings from about half of the coconut should be enough for this recipe; these larger shavings will be harder to measure by the cup. Scatter the shavings on a baking sheet and dry in the oven for about 30 minutes, then set aside to cool before proceeding with the recipe.

Aleppo Pepper Phyllo Crisps

Phyllo is rarely the star of the show. Though its thin layers and flaky texture are inherently showy, often the filling or topping ends up taking center stage. Not so here, where the thin sheets of pastry are layered with seasoned butter for a very simple, and very tasty, snack.

Phyllo is commonly available in the freezer section; allow time for it to thaw overnight in the refrigerator before using. Typically there are two well-sealed packages in a 1-pound box, so you can easily use half here and keep the rest frozen for another use. Sizes of the sheets can vary from one brand to the next; I used 9- by 12-inch sheets here. But the technique applies to any size sheets; you just may end up with varied numbers of servings, or you can cut the strips differently. | **Makes about 32 crisps**

$1/2$ cup unsalted butter

1 teaspoon ground Aleppo pepper or other moderately spicy chile powder

$1/2$ teaspoon kosher salt or flaky or coarse sea salt

8 ounces phyllo dough, thawed

Preheat the oven to 375°F. Line 2 baking sheets with parchment paper or silicone baking mats. Set 2 oven racks at the centermost positions.

Melt the butter in a small saucepan over medium heat. Stir in the pepper and salt and set aside to cool slightly.

Lay the stack of phyllo dough out flat on one side of the counter. Lift off the top sheet of dough and set it in front of you. Lightly but evenly brush the phyllo dough with a bit of the seasoned butter. Lift another piece of phyllo dough from the stack and lay it over the first, matching the edges as evenly as you can and pressing down well with your hands to adhere the two layers. Again lightly coat the surface of the dough with some of the seasoned butter. Continue layering and buttering the dough in the same fashion; you should end up with a stack about $1/4$ inch tall. The top layer of phyllo dough should remain unbuttered on top. Press well all over the surface with your palms to help make sure all the layers are well compacted.

Use a small sharp knife to halve the stack of phyllo lengthwise, then cut across into strips about $3/4$ inch wide. Or, you can instead form small squares, cutting the dough lengthwise in quarters and across into $1^{1}/2$ inch wide pieces. Arrange the phyllo pieces on the baking sheets.

Bake until lightly browned and crisp, 18 to 20 minutes, switching the pans halfway.

Set aside to cool on the baking sheet, then transfer the crisps to a plate or platter for serving. The crisps will be best the day they are baked.

This is a simple idea that has many possible variations.

Variation #1: Consider trying—in place of the Aleppo pepper—2 teaspoons of curry powder or 1 tablespoon finely minced tender fresh herbs (flat-leaf parsley, chives, and/or basil) and $1/4$ teaspoon finely minced or pressed garlic.

Variation #2: For a pesto variation, use $1/4$ cup melted unsalted butter and $1/4$ cup prepared pesto (pesto tends to contribute enough salt on its own, but you can add a pinch extra salt if you like).

Soy-Wasabi Wonton Crisps

Wonton skins get upgraded from mere vehicle for enclosing a savory filling to being the key figure in an addictive snack. The prepared version of wasabi paste is sold in tubes or tubs and keeps well for many months in the refrigerator. Or you can use wasabi powder from a tin and add just enough water to form a smooth paste. | **Makes 6 to 8 servings**

---

1 tablespoon prepared wasabi paste
1 tablespoon soy sauce
1 teaspoon toasted sesame oil
   Vegetable oil, for frying
24 wonton squares
1/4 cup minced fresh cilantro

Stir together the wasabi paste, soy sauce, and sesame oil in a small bowl to make a thin paste. The consistency should be thin enough to easily drizzle over the wonton crisps, so add a small amount of water, if needed. Set aside.

Pour about 2 inches of oil in a large heavy saucepan (the oil should not come more than halfway up the sides of the pan). Bring to 375°F over medium heat.

While the oil is heating, separate the wonton squares into 3 or 4 stacks and cut across each stack to make strips 1/2 inch wide. Separate the individual strips with your fingers. To test the oil, gently add 1 strip; it should bubble moderately and brown within 1 minute. Add about one-quarter of the wonton strips and stir very gently with a slotted spoon to be sure they're not sticking together. Fry until lightly browned and crisp, 30 to 60 seconds, then scoop them out to paper towels to drain. Continue frying the remaining wonton strips in batches, allowing the oil to reheat between batches as needed.

Put the fried wonton strips in a large bowl. Stir the wasabi mixture again and drizzle it over, tossing quickly but gently to evenly coat the strips. Sprinkle the cilantro over and toss gently again for a few moments.

The seasoned wonton crisps will be best served right away, though the strips can be fried up to 2 hours in advance and tossed with seasonings just before serving.

TOSSING

Sometimes I like to take the concept of "tossing" food more literally than others, and this is one of those times. The twisty, curly strips of fried wonton can be tough to stir evenly with a spoon or spatula, at least not without inadvertently crushing some of the strips. I find it easier to grab the bowl from both sides and toss the mixture a few inches up into the air and let it fall back into the bowl, which helps distribute the seasoning. An extra-large bowl is better, particularly while you're getting the hang of it. It's not only quick and a bit of fun, but in cases like this it does the most efficient job.

Pita Chips *with Hazelnut and Parmesan*

There are many possible variations on this simple theme of turning pita pocket bread into supremely snackable treats. Replace the Parmesan cheese here with blue cheese instead. Forgo the nuts and cheese altogether, and add minced parsley, chives, and rosemary to the butter/thyme combo for an herbal version. Or add a couple tablespoons each of mashed roasted garlic and minced sun-dried tomatoes to the softened butter for a more robust twist. I love this particular combination of rich Parmesan and toasty-earthy hazelnuts; it makes a crisp snack that's eminently enjoyable. | **Makes 32 chips**

¼ cup chopped hazelnuts

¼ cup freshly grated Parmesan cheese

2 teaspoons chopped fresh thyme

¼ cup unsalted butter, at room temperature

¼ teaspoon freshly ground black pepper

2 pocket pita breads

½ teaspoon kosher salt or flaky or coarse sea salt

Preheat the oven to 350°F.

Combine the hazelnuts, Parmesan cheese, and thyme in a food processor and pulse until the nuts are very finely chopped. Add the butter and pepper and pulse for 1 minute to make a smooth paste, scraping down the sides of the bowl as needed.

Use the tip of a small knife to split the edge of each pita bread and gently pull the 2 halves apart. Set the pita rounds inside-up on the counter and spread each with one quarter of the hazelnut mixture. Sprinkle the salt evenly over the top. Cut each round into eighths, like you're cutting a pie, and arrange them on a rimmed baking sheet. They can be pretty snug; alternating the triangles helps fit them on the baking sheet compactly.

Toast the pita pieces in the oven until lightly browned and crisp, 8 to 10 minutes.

Set aside to cool, then arrange on a platter or in a bowl for serving. If you are not serving right away, store them in an airtight container for up to 3 or 4 days.

Spicy Tortilla Crisps *with Queso Fundido*

Queso fundido (which translates from Spanish into one of the most appetizing phrases I know: melted cheese) is often served in the small cast-iron pan in which it is cooked, which keeps the cheese warm and melty. A 5-inch or 6-inch pan is ideal. Or you can make the cheese mixture in a small skillet and transfer it to a warmed small bowl for serving. If you have a small fondue pot, that's another good option. Rather than cutting corn tortillas pie-style to make broad wedges, I prefer to cut them crosswise on the diagonal into long, slender wedges. Spice the chips to suit your taste; chile-heads may wish to use hot chipotle, while ancho is a good choice for more moderate heat. Depending on the heat of the chile you use, the quantity needed may vary: Use a light dusting for hotter types, a more generous one for milder chile powder. | **Makes 4 to 6 servings**

---

2 tablespoons olive oil

4 small corn tortillas (6 inches in diameter)

1/2 to 1 teaspoon chile powder (such as chipotle or ancho)

1 teaspoon kosher salt or flaky or coarse sea salt

1/2 cup thinly sliced green onions, white and green portions

3/4 cup grated sharp cheddar cheese

3/4 cup grated Monterey Jack cheese

2 tablespoons chopped fresh cilantro

Preheat the oven to 375°F.

Use 1 tablespoon of the olive oil to lightly brush the tops of the corn tortillas, then sprinkle the chile powder and salt evenly over them (see page 14). Starting at either the left or right edge of a tortilla, cut a vertical strip that's about 1 inch at its widest point, at a slight angle. Moving inward, cut another long strip at a similar angle in the opposite direction. Continue zigzagging across the tortilla cutting long triangular strips that alternate between the point being downward and upward. (See photo, page iv.) Repeat with the remaining tortillas. You should get about 8 strips per tortilla. Arrange the strips on a rimmed baking sheet.

Toast in the oven until just crisped, 10 to 12 minutes. Set aside to cool. The crisps can be made a day ahead and stored in an airtight container.

Shortly before serving, heat the remaining 1 tablespoon of olive oil in a small, heavy skillet or pan, preferably cast iron, over medium heat. Add the green onions and cook, stirring often, until just tender but not browned, 2 to 3 minutes. Add the cheeses, a small handful at a time, stirring until each addition is almost fully melted before adding the next. When all the cheese has been added, continue cooking for a minute or two undisturbed so that the mixture gets nice and bubbly. Scatter the cilantro over the queso fundido and serve right away, with the tortilla crisps alongside.

Parmesan–Pink Peppercorn Crisps

Known as *frico* in Italy, these thin discs are little more than melted cheese that's been baked to the point of transformation from melty and soft to firm and crisp. The cheese alone is delicious enough as is, but I add a bit of seasoning for extra panache. Firm cheeses will provide the best results—Parmesan, aged Gouda, aged Manchego (see variations)—but feel free to play around with others. I recommend grating on the medium holes of a box grater, rather than finely grating the cheese, for this preparation. Instead of leaving the crisps flat for serving, you can slip them while warm onto a rolling pin or side of a small jar, so they cool and set in a curved shape.

I love the slightly floral/fruity flavor of pink peppercorns, a tasty foil for the Parmesan cheese. Pink peppercorns are not as brittle as black peppercorns, so they're a bit tough to crush in a mortar and pestle. Instead, my favorite tool for this is a mini food processor or spice grinder (see page 10). | **Makes 12 crisps**

---

1 cup freshly grated Parmesan cheese
1 teaspoon ground pink peppercorns

Preheat the oven to 400°F. Line a rimmed baking sheet with parchment paper or a silicone baking mat.

In a small bowl, toss together the Parmesan and ground pink peppercorns until evenly blended. Spoon a slightly rounded tablespoon of the cheese mixture onto the baking sheet, using the back of the spoon to spread it out to an even circle about 3 inches across. Repeat to form 12 circles total.

Bake until just lightly browned around the edges and melted together, 3 to 5 minutes.

Let the crisps cool on the baking sheets for a few minutes, then use a metal spatula to carefully transfer them to a wire rack topped with paper towel to cool completely. If you are not serving within an hour or two, store the crisps in an airtight container for 1 to 2 days.

Variation #1: Use 1 cup grated aged gouda and 1 teaspoon whole cumin seeds in place of the Parmesan and pink peppercorns. Proceed as noted, but form smaller circles of cheese, about 2 inches across, as this cheese tends to be more delicate when melted.

Variation #2: Use 1 cup grated aged manchego and 1 tablespoon finely minced green olives in place of the Parmesan and pink peppercorns. Proceed as noted, but form smaller circles of cheese, about 2 inches across, as this cheese tends to be more delicate when melted.

Anchovy Crisps

This is an unapologetically retro recipe, no doubt, and one that isn't shy about its ho-hum appearance either, but it's one I love. The delicate crispness that comes from the simple combination of white bread and butter and the salty-brisk flavor of anchovies is a delight, a quick little snack idea for tonight's cocktail hour. For an even quicker version, spread the anchovy butter on slices of baguette and toast just until lightly browned.

Anchovy paste, usually sold in a toothpaste-like tube, works best here. But you can use 3 to 4 anchovy fillets instead, blending them very well with the butter to make as smooth a mixture as you can. | **Makes 6 to 8 servings**

---

10 slices white sandwich bread

$1/4$ cup unsalted butter, at room temperature

2 tablespoons anchovy paste

Preheat the oven to 400°F. Line 2 rimmed baking sheets with parchment paper or silicone baking mats. Set 2 oven racks at the center-most positions.

Cut the crusts from the bread, squaring off the slices as you do. (Bread trim can be whirled in a food processor to make bread crumbs for another use.) Working with 1 slice at a time, roll a rolling pin over the bread slices a few times to evenly flatten them.

Combine the butter and anchovy paste in a small bowl and mash them together with the tines of a fork until smooth and evenly blended.

Spread about $1^1/2$ teaspoons of the anchovy butter over each flattened square of bread, then cut the square diagonally into 2 triangles. Arrange the triangles on the baking sheets.

Toast in the oven until crisp and lightly browned around the edges, 8 to 10 minutes, switching the pans about halfway through.

Let cool, then arrange on a plate or serving platter. These crisps are best served shortly after toasting.

Breads and Pastries

What a versatile category this is, with recipes based on classic foundations from which endless possibilities can spring. Slices of toasted baguette, puff pastry, buttery pastry dough, quick breads, and flat breads can be embellished in innumerable ways. After you've been through a recipe once or twice, have fun playing around with alternatives: black pepper instead of basil in the *grissini* (page 58) or sun-dried tomatoes instead of bacon in the Bacon-Chive Bread with Goat Cheese (page 47). Add roasted garlic (page 149) to the topping for the Crostini with Pine Nuts and Mint Ricotta (page 41). Follow your whims. The different dough and bread bases can serve as foundations to which simple seasoning changes or ingredient swaps can be done without affecting the overall outcome of the recipe.

Snacking Croutons

Do you tend to load up on croutons at the salad bar, sampling some on the way back to your table? Or snag a few from the bag to nibble on before scattering croutons over greens at home? I know I do. Here's a recipe in praise of the crouton's natural snack-worthiness, meant to be enjoyed as is. Though if you simply must, you can sprinkle them over a green salad, too.

If the bread you're using has a texture dense enough to hold up well in cubes when fresh, go for it. But if the loaf has a softer texture inside, it may be best to wait until a day or two after you buy it before cutting it into cubes. In a pinch, you can cut the bread into 1-inch slices and leave them on a wire rack for a few hours to dry out a bit. This is not a great recipe for using a baguette; I don't think its high crust-to-crumb ratio is ideal for croutons. | **Makes 6 to 8 servings**

1/3 cup unsalted butter, melted

1 tablespoon Worcestershire sauce

2 teaspoons minced fresh thyme, or 1 teaspoon dried

1 teaspoon Dijon mustard

1 teaspoon minced or pressed garlic

1/2 teaspoon kosher salt or flaky or coarse sea salt

1/4 teaspoon freshly ground black pepper

12 ounces rustic bread, cut into 1-inch cubes (about 8 cups)

Preheat the oven to 350°F.

Combine the melted butter, Worcestershire sauce, thyme, mustard, garlic, salt, and pepper in a large bowl and stir well to mix. Add the bread cubes and toss well for a minute or two to thoroughly and evenly coat the bread cubes with the seasoning ingredients. Scatter the bread cubes in an even layer on a rimmed baking sheet.

Bake until evenly browned and crisp, 15 to 17 minutes, stirring the cubes two or three times to help them toast evenly. The croutons should be just crisp, but not hard, so they're easy to enjoy as a snack.

Let cool completely on the baking sheet, then transfer the croutons to a serving bowl. They will be best served on the same day they are made.

Crostini *with Pine Nuts and Mint Ricotta*

Crostini ("little toasts" in Italian) are the blank white canvas of salty snacks, the perfect starting point for any number of options. It can be as simple as topping them with your favorite cheese, top-notch prosciutto, diced tomatoes tossed with balsamic vinegar, chicken liver mousse—you name it. This variation is a light and flavorful option, with ricotta cheese, toasty pine nuts, and fresh mint. Landjaeger, a recommended optional addition, is a type of lightly smoked dried sausage that adds a dash of savory richness to the crostini. | **Makes 6 to 8 servings**

- 1 cup whole milk ricotta
- 24 slices baguette
- 2 tablespoons olive oil
- 1 clove garlic
- 1/4 cup pine nuts, toasted
- 2 tablespoons minced fresh mint
- 1/4 teaspoon kosher salt or flaky or coarse sea salt
- 24 thin slices landjaeger (optional)

If the ricotta you're using shows any excess water around the edges, drain it in a fine-mesh sieve for about 30 minutes.

Preheat the oven to 400°F.

Arrange the baguette slices on a rimmed baking sheet and toast in the oven until lightly browned and crisp, 8 to10 minutes. Set aside to cool; then brush each slice lightly with olive oil and rub the garlic clove once or twice on each slice.

Stir together the ricotta, pine nuts, mint, and salt in a small bowl. Spread the ricotta mixture onto the crostini and top each with a thin slice of landjaeger. Serve right away.

Black *and* White Puff Sticks

Puff pastry is one of the cook's ultimate snack-friendly shortcuts. Just the slightest embellishment before cutting and baking produces an elegant, tasty treat to nibble on. I use seeds here, but it could just as well have been chile powder, finely grated cheese, chopped olives, or any other number of options.

Since puff pastry is most often sold frozen, you'll want to plan ahead so it can thaw slowly in the refrigerator overnight. If you can find all-butter puff pastry dough, all the better. Some bakeries sell it, as do specialty food shops and well-stocked grocery stores. | **Makes about 16 puff sticks**

---

1 sheet (about 8 ounces) puff pastry, thawed

1 large egg

$1/2$ teaspoon kosher salt or flaky or coarse sea salt, plus more for egg wash

2 tablespoons white sesame seeds

2 tablespoons poppy seeds or black sesame seeds

Preheat the oven to 375°F. Line a rimmed baking sheet with parchment paper or a silicone baking mat.

Lay the puff pastry out on a lightly floured work surface and lightly dust the top of the dough with flour. Roll the dough into a rectangle about 10 inches by 12 inches, trying to keep the edges as even as possible.

Beat the egg well in a small bowl, then beat in a pinch of the salt. Lightly brush the surface of the puff pastry with a thin sheen of the beaten egg. Sprinkle the sesame seeds evenly over the dough, pressing down on them a bit to help them adhere. Season evenly with

$1/4$ teaspoon of the salt. Carefully flip the pastry over and lightly brush the other side with egg. Sprinkle the poppy seeds evenly over this second side of the dough, pressing down a bit to help them adhere. Season evenly with the remaining $1/4$ teaspoon of the salt.

Use the rolling blade of a pizza cutter or pastry wheel (plain or fluted) to cut the dough crosswise into $3/4$-inch strips. Lift one of the strips and twist the ends three or four times, then lay the twisted strip on the baking sheet. Repeat with the remaining strips, arranging them about $1/2$ inch apart.

Bake until lightly browned and crisp, 12 to 15 minutes.

Let cool slightly on the baking sheet, then arrange upright in a jar or on a platter to serve. If you are not serving within a few hours, store the sticks in an airtight container for up to 2 days.

Cornbread-Chile "Biscotti"

Not nearly as hard and crunchy as traditional sweet biscotti, this variation on the theme twice-bakes chile-studded cornbread to enhance the nutty character of the cornmeal. It's a snack that lingers somewhere between cornbread and cracker. A great accompaniment to these biscotti is the Black Bean Dip (page 145). Or for a more substantial snack, consider topping the biscotti with a bit of pulled pork or carnitas. Two poblano chiles should be just about right to get the 1/2 cup diced chiles needed here, if you choose to go the fresh route. | **Makes about 40 biscotti**

---

1 1/2 cups fine yellow cornmeal

1/2 cup all-purpose flour

1 tablespoon baking powder

2 teaspoons sugar

1 teaspoon kosher salt or flaky or coarse sea salt

3 large eggs

1 cup whole milk

1/2 cup unsalted butter, melted

1/2 cup diced roasted chiles, fresh (see page 14) or canned

Preheat the oven to 375°F. Butter an 8- or 9-inch square cake pan.

Combine the cornmeal, flour, baking powder, sugar, and salt in a large bowl and stir with a whisk to evenly blend. Make a well in the center.

Whisk the eggs in a medium bowl to blend them well, then gradually whisk in the milk and melted butter. Pour these wet ingredients into the well in the dry ingredients and add the chiles. Gently stir with the whisk just until the ingredients are evenly blended. Pour the batter into the prepared pan.

Bake until a toothpick inserted in the center comes out clean, about 20 minutes. Set aside on a wire rack to cool slightly, then turn the cornbread out onto the rack and let cool completely. The cornbread can be made up to 2 days ahead and well wrapped in foil.

Using a serrated knife, trim away the crust from the 4 sides of the cornbread and save them for a snack (or dice and toast them to use as croutons on your next green salad). Cut the bread into 1/2-inch-thick slices, then cut each slice crosswise into thirds.

Reheat the oven to 350°F. Set 2 oven racks at the centermost positions.

Lay the cornbread slices (they can be snug but avoid overlapping) on 2 rimmed baking sheets. Bake just until lightly browned around the edges and crisped, about 1 hour, turning the slices and switching the pans after 30 minutes.

Transfer the cornbread biscotti to a wire rack to cool completely. The biscotti are best served the day they are baked.

Cheddar Ale Bread

It has long been said that bread and beer are kindred spirits, both made from grain, water, and yeast—the processes by which they are made differing just enough so that one produces a light loaf, the other a frothy pint. Here they meld more directly, the yeasty character of ale contributing flavor and lightness to the loaf. The cheese adds delicious flavor, with the slightest hint of smokiness from smoked paprika. Lighter ales will be best here, rather than a hoppy IPA. You can even make the bread with a can of run-of-the-mill lager with good results. This is one of those easy quick breads that can have you enjoying a fresh-baked salty snack in much the same way a batch of banana bread fulfills that afternoon need for something sweet.
| **Makes 1 loaf (8 to 10 slices)**

2$1/2$ cups all-purpose flour

1$1/2$ cups grated sharp cheddar cheese

2 teaspoons baking powder

1$1/2$ teaspoons smoked paprika

1$1/2$ teaspoons kosher salt or flaky or coarse sea salt

1 (12-ounce) bottle pale ale

Preheat the oven to 400°F. Generously butter a 9 by 5-inch loaf pan.

Stir together the flour, cheese, baking powder, paprika, and salt in a large bowl, breaking up any clumps of the cheese so that it is well distributed with the flour. Add the ale all at once and stir gently but quickly just until blended. It's okay if there are a couple of lumps; avoid overmixing. Spoon the batter into the prepared loaf pan, smoothing the top.

Bake the bread until lightly browned on top and a toothpick inserted in the center comes out clean, 35 to 40 minutes.

Let the bread cool for a few minutes in the pan, then turn it out onto a wire rack to cool completely. Cut into slices to serve, or wrap well in foil for up to 2 days before serving.

Bacon-Chive Bread *with Goat Cheese*

This savory bread is not only a great snack (perfect as a carry-along, for a picnic or hike), it also makes a great addition to your brunch menu on those lazy weekend mornings. | **Makes 12 to 16 servings**

---

6 slices thick-cut bacon

2 cups all-purpose flour

1 teaspoon baking powder

3/4 teaspoon baking soda

1/2 teaspoon kosher salt or flaky or coarse
    sea salt

1/4 teaspoon freshly ground black pepper

1 1/2 cups (about 6 ounces) finely crumbled fresh
    plain goat cheese

1/2 cup unsalted butter, at room temperature

2 large eggs

1 cup whole milk

1/3 cup chopped fresh chives

Heat a large skillet over medium heat. Add the bacon slices and cook, turning the slices over every couple of minutes, until nicely browned and crisp, 8 to 10 minutes. Transfer the bacon to paper towels to drain and cool. When cooled, crumble or cut the bacon into small pieces; set aside.

Preheat the oven to 350°F. Butter and flour an 8- or 9-inch round cake pan.

Combine the flour, baking powder, baking soda, salt, and pepper in a medium bowl and stir well to mix.

Combine 1 1/4 cups of the goat cheese and the butter in the bowl of a stand mixer fitted with the paddle attachment and beat at medium speed until smooth. Add one of the eggs and beat until fully incorporated, then beat in the second egg, scraping down the sides of the bowl as needed. Gradually add the dry ingredients with the mixer at low speed, alternating with the milk. Take the bowl from the stand and stir in the bacon and chives by hand, just until incorporated. Spoon the batter into the prepared pan, smoothing the top. Sprinkle the remaining 1/4 cup of goat cheese over the top.

Bake until the top is lightly browned and the bread pulls away from the sides of the pan, 35 to 40 minutes. Let cool slightly in the pan, then turn the bread out onto the rack to cool completely, inverting the bread so that the goat cheese topping is upright.

Cut the cooled bread into 12 to 16 wedges, arrange on a platter or large plate, and serve. The bread will keep for 1 day, well wrapped in foil.

Stilton *and* Walnut Pinwheels

A quick pastry dough serves as a great foundation for any number of salty snacks. I top it with a favorite duo of mine—blue cheese and walnuts—for a flavorful treat. In place of the Stilton, other blue cheeses can be used, such as Gorgonzola or Roquefort. | **Makes about 3 dozen**

Pastry Dough

- 1¹/2 cups all-purpose flour
- ¹/2 teaspoon kosher salt or flaky or coarse sea salt
- ¹/2 cup unsalted butter, cut into pieces and chilled
- 1 large egg yolk
- 4 tablespoons ice water, plus more if needed

Filling

- ¹/2 cup toasted walnuts
- ³/4 cup crumbled Stilton cheese or other blue cheese, at room temperature
- ¹/4 cup cream cheese, at room temperature
- 2 tablespoons finely chopped chives
- Kosher salt or flaky or coarse sea salt (optional)

To make the dough, combine the flour and salt in a food processor and pulse once to mix. Add the butter and egg yolk and pulse until the mixture has a coarse sandy texture. Drizzle the water in 1 tablespoon at a time, pulsing a few times after each addition. Avoid overmixing or the dough will be tough rather than flaky. It may not form a ball in the machine, but it has the proper amount of liquid if squeezing some of the dough between your fingers feels no longer dusty dry. Turn the dough out onto a work surface, form it into a disk, and wrap in plastic. Refrigerate for at least 30 minutes.

Preheat the oven to 350°F. Line a rimmed baking sheet with parchment paper or a silicone baking mat.

To make the filling, put the walnuts in a food processor and pulse until finely chopped. Add the Stilton and cream cheese and pulse until well blended, scraping down the sides as needed. Transfer the mixture to a small bowl and stir in the chives. Add a bit of salt if needed (saltiness will depend on the type of cheese used).

Roll the dough out on a lightly floured work surface to a rectangle about 10 by 14 inches, with a thickness of about ¹/8 inch. Spread the Stilton mixture evenly over the dough, leaving a 1-inch strip along one long edge blank. Brush the exposed dough lightly with water. Starting at the edge opposite the blank edge, roll the dough in a snug log, pressing gently on the moistened edge to help it adhere to the dough. Wrap the log in plastic and chill until firm enough to slice easily, 30 to 45 minutes.

With a small sharp knife, cut across the log into slices about ¹/4 inch thick. Arrange the slices on the baking sheet with about ¹/2 inch between them. Bake until nicely browned, about 25 minutes. Let cool on the baking sheet, then transfer to a plate or bowl for serving, or store in an airtight container for up to 3 days.

Porcini Choux Puffs

Choux pastry is a great building-block recipe to have in your repertoire. The versatile dough can be used in so many ways, from cheesy gougères to sweet profiteroles. In this recipe, I infuse a subtle touch of wild mushroom using finely ground dried porcini mushrooms, made by tearing $1/2$ ounce of dried porcini into small pieces, then whirling them in my all-purpose spice/seed grinder (see page 10) until finely ground. (You can also find porcini powder in specialty shops or online.)

When piping out the dough, you may end up with little points when you lift up the piping bag. I seldom fuss over these, particularly when making choux puffs for snacking. But for a tidier finish when you want a more polished look, you can gently smooth down any points with the back of a small spoon. I prefer not to brush choux with egg wash. | **Makes about 3 dozen puffs**

---

1 cup water

2 tablespoons powdered dry porcini
    mushrooms (see headnote)

$1/2$ cup unsalted butter, cut into pieces

1 teaspoon kosher salt or flaky or coarse
    sea salt

1 cup all-purpose flour

3 large eggs

Preheat the oven to 400°F. Line 2 baking sheets with parchment paper or silicone baking mats.

Stir together the water and porcini powder in a saucepan and bring just to a low boil over medium-high heat. Reduce the heat to medium-low, add the butter and salt, and stir gently with a wooden spoon until the butter is melted. Add the flour and stir gently until fully incorporated. Continue to stir, a bit more vigorously, until a smooth dough forms that pulls away from the sides of the pan, about 1 minute longer.

Take the pan from the heat and add one of the eggs. (To help avoid getting any shell in the dough, you can first break the egg into a ramekin or other small dish and remove any stray shell bits.) As soon as the egg is added, stir well to blend fully into the dough. Add the remaining eggs one at a time.

Spoon the dough into a pastry bag fitted with a $3/4$-inch plain tip. Pipe into rounds of about $1^1/2$ inches in diameter on one of the lined baking sheets, with 1 inch between them. When that baking sheet is filled, bake until nicely browned and well puffed, about 20 minutes. Shortly before the first tray is done, pipe the remaining dough into the second baking sheet. When the first sheet of puffs is done, bake the second sheet.

Let cool for a few minutes on the baking sheets, then transfer to a wire rack. Arrange the choux on a platter or in a basket for serving. The puffs will be best served shortly after baking.

Buckwheat Biscuits *with Ham and Pear*

When I was a kid, my sister and I took a trip east with our mom to visit some of her family. After spending time with part of the clan in Columbus, Mississippi, cousin Judy sent us off in our rental car with a big foil packet of freshly made biscuits that were sandwiched with salty, bold slices of country ham. Now, I don't claim to have any Southern biscuit heritage coursing through my veins today, so the departure to a buckwheat biscuit—purely for the nutty flavor of that flour—and perhaps not classically Southern technique will hopefully be forgiven. But this recipe is an homage to the indelible memory of the perfect road trip snack we shared that summer. | **Makes 24 biscuits**

1¹⁄₂ cups all-purpose flour

¹⁄₂ cup buckwheat flour

1 tablespoon baking powder

1 teaspoon kosher salt or flaky or coarse sea salt

¹⁄₂ cup unsalted butter, cut into pieces and chilled

1 cup whole milk

4 ounces sliced dry-cured ham (such as country ham, Serrano ham, or prosciutto)

¹⁄₂ ripe but firm pear, cored and sliced

Preheat the oven to 400°F. Line 2 baking sheets with parchment paper or silicone baking mats. Set 2 oven racks at the centermost positions.

Combine the all-purpose flour, buckwheat flour, baking powder, and salt in a food processor and pulse once or twice to blend. Add the butter and pulse until it is finely chopped and the mixture has the texture of coarse cornmeal.

Transfer the mixture to a bowl, add the milk, and gently stir until the dough is just evenly mixed; avoid overmixing. Use 2 large spoons to drop the dough on the baking sheets by heaping tablespoons into mounds about 2 inches across (about 24 biscuits in all).

Bake until puffed and lightly browned, 20 to 22 minutes, switching the pans halfway through. Transfer the biscuits to a wire rack to cool.

Cut each cooled biscuit in half horizontally. Halve or otherwise portion the slices of ham and pear so that they'll fit easily onto the biscuits and sandwich each biscuit with some of each. Serve right away.

Semolina Waffles *with Caramelized Onion*

I don't indulge in them nearly as much as I might like, but I really do love waffles. It's fun playing around with them for dinner and dessert as much as for breakfast. Though a tasty nibble all on its own, this waffle also serves as a great base for cheese, particularly a rich blue cheese. And I've been known to sandwich scrambled egg between wedges of the waffle, too. Tasty.

| **Makes 8 to 12 servings**

6 tablespoons unsalted butter

1 1/2 cups thinly sliced yellow onion

3/4 cup all-purpose flour

3/4 cup semolina flour

1 1/2 teaspoons baking soda

1 teaspoon kosher salt or flaky or coarse sea salt

1 1/4 cups buttermilk

2 large eggs, separated

Melt 2 tablespoons of the butter in a medium skillet over medium heat. Add the onion and cook, stirring occasionally, until tender and aromatic, 3 to 4 minutes. Top the onion with a piece of parchment paper or foil, reduce the heat to low, and cook gently until they are soft and evenly caramelized, stirring occasionally, about 30 minutes. Set aside to cool.

Melt the remaining 4 tablespoons of butter in a small saucepan over medium heat; set aside to cool. Preheat a waffle iron to medium-high heat.

Stir together the all-purpose flour, semolina flour, baking soda, and salt in a large bowl. In a medium bowl, gently whisk together the buttermilk, melted butter, and egg yolks until smooth. Add the wet ingredients and the caramelized onions to the dry ingredients and stir gently just to mix.

Beat the egg whites in a stand mixer fitted with the whip attachment at medium speed or by hand with a large whisk until soft peaks form. Add about one third of the egg whites to the batter and use a rubber spatula to briskly fold them in to lighten the batter; then, more gently, fold in the remaining egg whites.

Pour a generous 1/2 cup of the batter onto the waffle iron (more or less depending on the size of your iron). Close the waffle iron and cook until lightly browned and the steam subsides, 5 to 6 minutes. Set aside on a wire rack to cool. Continue making waffles with the remaining batter.

Cut the cooled waffles into wedges or squares and arrange them on a plate or platter for serving. They will be best served shortly after they're made.

Olive Focaccia *with Lemon*

Picholine olives are a great option here, though you can use other types of good green olives instead, or even good black olives, if you prefer. The sharpness of the lemon slices mellows a bit with the baking, adding nice tang of contrast to the rich olive bread. When Meyer lemons are available, they'd be a great choice to use here. There are countless ways you can vary the recipe. In place of the lemon slices, you could instead top the bread with grated Parmesan cheese, herb salt, or a scattering of thinly sliced red onion. | **Makes 18 portions**

---

2 cups all-purpose flour, plus more if needed

1 teaspoon kosher salt or flaky or coarse sea salt, plus more for sprinkling

1/4 teaspoon freshly ground black pepper

1/2 cup warm (105° to 110°F) water

2 teaspoons (1 envelope) active dry yeast

2 tablespoons freshly squeezed lemon juice

1/2 cup finely chopped green olives

2 large lemons

2 tablespoons olive oil

Combine the flour, salt, and pepper in the bowl of a stand mixer fitted with the paddle attachment and blend for a few moments to mix. Form a well in the center of the flour, pour in the warm water, and scatter the yeast over, stirring it in gently. Let sit until the yeast is frothy, about 5 minutes. Blend the wet and dry ingredients together at medium-low speed, drizzling in the lemon juice as you go. When a cohesive dough forms, add the olives and continue blending for 1 to 2 minutes to incorporate them into the dough; depending on how moist the olives are, you may find the dough to be on the sticky side, so add a bit more flour if needed. Turn the dough out onto

a lightly floured work surface and knead it for 2 to 3 minutes to form a satiny dough.

Transfer the dough to a lightly oiled bowl, turning the dough so it is evenly coated. Cover the bowl with a kitchen towel and set aside in a warm place until doubled in bulk, about 1 hour. Turn the dough out onto a lightly oiled baking sheet and punch it down, using your fingers and the heel of your hand to press it into a rectangle about 9 by 12 inches. If the dough begins to spring back quite a lot as you're trying to spread it out, take a break for a few minutes and let the dough rest; it'll then be a little more cooperative. Cover the dough with the towel and set aside again until nearly doubled in bulk, about 30 minutes.

Preheat the oven to 400°F.

While the dough is rising, use your sharpest knife to cut the lemons into very thin slices. If you have a mandoline slicer that has a particularly sharp blade, you may be able to do this on the mandoline, but I find my mandoline sometimes mashes the tender flesh rather than cutting cleanly through it. Discard any seeds as you come to them. You'll want about 24 slices.

When the dough is risen, brush the top lightly with the olive oil. Arrange the lemon slices on the dough in 3 lengthwise rows of slightly overlapping slices, the rows evenly spaced across the width of the dough. Sprinkle salt lightly and evenly over the top.

Bake the bread until both the bread and the lemon slices are lightly browned, about 20 minutes. Let cool for a few minutes in the pan, then slip the bread onto a wire rack to cool completely.

Use a serrated knife to cut 3 strips lengthwise (ideally the lemon slices will run down the center of each of those strips), then crosswise into 2-inch pieces. Arrange the bread on a platter and serve. The bread will be best on the day it is made.

PITTING OLIVES

When you're going to chop olives for a recipe, here's a great way to first coax the pit from the olive. Just lay the broad flat side of a chef's knife directly on the olive and, while holding the knife securely with one hand, (carefully!) press down firmly on the top of the blade with the palm of your other hand. This should split the flesh of the olive and expose the pit for easy removal. For any uncooperative olives, simply cut the flesh away from the pit with a small knife.

Mustard Soft Pretzels

The quintessential sidekick to a good soft pretzel is a dish of flavorful mustard. But it's not used for dunking in this case: Rustic grainy mustard is added to the pretzel dough itself for a dose of savory flavor.

Malt powder is not necessarily a traditional pretzel ingredient, though malt syrup is often used and adds an interesting dimension of character. I've tried pretzels with both, and while the malt syrup version may be more classic, the malt powder version works well. And the rest of the jar is great to have on hand for adding an accent to a bowl of ice cream for dessert!

| **Makes 12 pretzels**

3 cups all-purpose flour, plus more if needed

3 tablespoons malt powder

$1\frac{1}{2}$ teaspoons kosher salt or flaky or coarse sea salt, plus more for sprinkling

1 cup warm water (105° to 110°F)

2 teaspoons (1 envelope) active dry yeast

3 tablespoons grainy mustard

1 tablespoon baking soda

1 large egg yolk

$1\frac{1}{2}$ teaspoons water

Combine the flour, malt powder, and kosher salt in the bowl of a stand mixer fitted with the paddle attachment and blend for a few moments to mix. Form a well in the center of the flour, pour in the warm water, and scatter the yeast over, stirring it in gently. Let sit until the yeast is frothy, about 5 minutes. Add the mustard to the bowl and blend the wet and dry ingredients together at medium-low speed until a cohesive dough forms. Turn the dough out onto a lightly floured work surface and knead it for 2 to 3 minutes, until smooth.

(Different types of mustard have varying levels of moisture; you may need to add a bit more flour if the dough is sticky.)

Transfer the dough to a lightly oiled bowl, turning the dough so it is evenly coated. Cover the bowl with a kitchen towel and set aside in a warm place until doubled in bulk, about 1 hour.

Preheat the oven to 375°F. Line a rimmed baking sheet with parchment paper or a silicone baking mat. Fill a large, broad saucepan about two-thirds full with water and set it over medium heat to warm while forming the pretzels. (If the water comes to a boil before needed, reduce the heat to low.)

Turn the risen dough out onto the counter and punch it down. Cut the dough into quarters, then cut each quarter into thirds, for 12 pieces of relatively even size. Cover the dough pieces with a kitchen towel until needed.

continued on next page

Roll one of the dough portions into a rope about 18 inches long. With the rope horizontal on the counter in front of you, lift up one end in each hand and draw the ends downward toward you, forming a broad loop with the ends overlapping at the bottom by about 2 inches. Cross your hands in front of you and pick up the two ends of dough, lifting them a couple inches above the counter. Cross your hands back to the left and right sides, twisting

the dough as you do. Lay the dough ends up over the top of the loop, so that the twist sits in the center of the pretzel. Gently pinch the dough ends down into the loop.

Set the pretzel aside, covered with a kitchen towel, while forming the remaining pretzels.

When all the pretzels have been formed, adjust the heat under the water to maintain a gentle simmer. Stir in the baking soda. Gently add 3 of the pretzels and simmer for 2 minutes, turning them halfway through. Lift the pretzels with a slotted spoon or spatula and drain for a few moments over the pan, then transfer to the prepared baking sheet. Simmer the remaining pretzels in the same fashion.

Beat the egg yolk with the $1^1/_2$ teaspoons water in a small dish. Brush the pretzels with the yolk mixture and sprinkle with coarse salt. Bake until golden brown, 20 to 25 minutes. Transfer the pretzels to a wire rack to cool.

Arrange the pretzels in a bowl or on a platter and serve. The pretzels will be at their best the day they are made. Should you have leftovers, they can be stored in an airtight container for a day or two, then warmed gently in the oven, wrapped in foil, to soften them up a bit.

Dilled Flatbread

A great snack as is, this thin version of focaccia can double as a base for slices of smoked salmon or other smoked fish, salmon rillettes (page 93), or pickled trout (page 97). Dill seed is one of those spices most of us don't get around to using very often. If you have a tin on your shelf that's been there since, oh, Bill Clinton was president, it may be time to swap it for a new supply. I like buying spices from the bulk section at a grocery store or in small quantities from a spice shop, so I can avoid buying more than I can use in a matter of months. | **Makes about 24 pieces**

1½ cups all-purpose flour, more if needed

1½ teaspoons kosher salt or flaky or coarse sea salt

¼ teaspoon freshly ground black pepper

½ cup warm water (105° to 110°F)

1 teaspoon (½ envelope) active dry yeast

3 tablespoons olive oil

⅓ cup finely chopped fresh dill

1½ teaspoons dill seed

Put the flour, 1 teaspoon of the salt, and the pepper in a medium bowl and stir to mix; then make a well in the center. Pour the warm water into the well and sprinkle the yeast over, stirring it in gently. Let sit until the yeast is frothy, about 5 minutes.

Stir together the wet and dry ingredients for a few seconds, then drizzle 2 tablespoons of the olive oil over and add the fresh dill. Continue to stir until a cohesive dough forms. Knead the dough on a lightly floured work surface until it becomes smooth and satiny, 2 to 3 minutes, adding a bit more flour if needed. Put the dough in a lightly oiled bowl (it could be the same bowl you mixed the dough in) and turn it to evenly but lightly coat the dough with oil. Cover the bowl with a kitchen towel and set aside in a warm place until the dough has doubled in bulk, 1 to 1¼ hours.

Preheat the oven to 375°F. Lightly oil a rimmed baking sheet.

Turn the risen dough out onto a lightly floured work surface and punch it down. Roll the dough out into a rectangle about the size of your baking sheet; when the dough begins to spring back quite a lot, let it rest for a few minutes before continuing to roll it out. Carefully transfer the dough to the baking sheet. Cover the pan with the towel and set aside in a warm place to rise by about half, about 45 minutes.

Stir together the dill seed and the remaining ½ teaspoon salt in a small dish. Uncover the dough, drizzle the remaining 1 tablespoon of olive oil over and brush it evenly over the dough. Sprinkle the dill-salt mixture evenly over and bake the bread until lightly browned on top, 15 to 18 minutes. Let cool on a wire rack.

Cut the bread into thirds lengthwise and across into strips about 2 inches wide. Arrange the pieces on a platter or tray and serve. The bread will be best on the day it is baked.

Basil Grissini

Grissini are those elegant, extrathin bread sticks, so crisp and inviting that it's hard to resist having just . . . one . . . more. A dose of fresh basil here adds a touch of bright flavor. These are ideal solo as a nibble to accompany cocktails, or perfect served alongside a bowl of tomato soup or cioppino. | **Makes 6 to 7 dozen** *grissini*

---

2 cups all-purpose flour, plus more if needed

1/3 cup finely chopped fresh basil

1 teaspoon kosher salt or flaky or coarse sea salt, plus more for sprinkling

1/2 cup warm water (105° to 110°F)

1 teaspoon (1/2 envelope) active dry yeast

2 tablespoons olive oil, plus more for brushing

Put the flour, basil, and salt in a medium bowl and stir to mix; then make a well in the center. Pour the warm water into the well and sprinkle the yeast over, stirring it in gently. Let sit until the yeast is frothy, about 5 minutes.

Stir the dough for a few moments with a wooden spoon, drawing in the flour from the edges, then drizzle the olive oil over the dough. Continue to stir the dough until it begins to come together in a ball. Transfer it to a lightly floured work surface and knead the dough until it becomes smooth and satiny, 2 to 3 minutes, adding a bit more flour if needed. Put the dough in a lightly oiled bowl (it could be the same bowl you mixed the dough in) and turn it to evenly but lightly coat the dough with

oil. Cover the bowl with a kitchen towel and set aside in a warm place until the dough has doubled in bulk, about 1 hour.

Preheat the oven to 375°F. Line 2 baking sheets with parchment paper or silicone baking mats.

Turn the risen dough out onto a lightly floured work surface and punch it down. Cut the dough into 4 even portions. Roll 1 portion out to a rectangle about 10 inches by 6 inches; the dough should be about 1/8 inch thick. When the dough begins to spring back quite a lot, let it rest for a minute or two before continuing.

Lightly brush the top of the dough with olive oil and sprinkle lightly with salt. Use the rolling blade of a pizza cutter or pasta wheel (preferably plain, not fluted) to cut the dough lengthwise into strips 1/4 inch wide. Arrange the strips on a prepared baking sheet, about 1/2 inch apart. Continue rolling and cutting 1 portion of dough at a time. When 1 baking sheet is filled, bake until the *grissini* are lightly but evenly browned and crisp, 8 to 10 minutes, while you continue filling the other baking sheet. Keep an eye on the progress nearing the end of baking; some of the thinner strips may be done sooner than others, so transfer them to a wire rack to cool while you continue baking the remaining *grissini* a minute or two longer. Continue with the remaining dough portions until all the *grissini* have been formed and baked, filling one sheet while another is baking. Ideally the baking sheets should cool off before new *grissini* are added.

When all of the *grissini* are cooled, transfer them to a basket for serving, or arrange the *grissini* in a couple of tall glasses. If not serving within a few hours, store in an airtight container for up to 3 days.

Seedy Cornmeal Bread Sticks

One thing I've learned from experts in gluten-free baking is that while traditional baking can be as simple as wheat flour, water, and salt, when you take gluten out of the equation it's necessary to blend different flours: some of the grain/nut type (such as rice, sorghum, cornmeal, almond, millet, amaranth) and some of the starch type (cornstarch, potato starch, tapioca flour). Together they provide the body, density, flavor, and other characteristics that generally mimic wheat-based flour.

Gluten-free kitchens are usually well stocked with a slew of different flours for just this purpose. For gluten-eating households, think of it as an opportunity to expand your culinary horizons. Consider integrating some of those interesting grain flours in your baking to expand your repertoire. Check the label of the cornmeal you're using to ensure it's gluten-free (reading ingredient lists is always a good habit when being gluten-free is critical). | **Makes 16 breadsticks**

---

1 cup fine yellow cornmeal

3/4 cup white sorghum flour

3/4 cup sweet (white) rice flour

1/2 cup plus 2 tablespoons cornstarch

1 tablespoon sugar

1 1/2 teaspoons kosher salt or flaky or coarse sea salt

3/4 cup warm (105° to 110°F) water

2 teaspoons (1 envelope) active dry yeast

2 large eggs, lightly beaten

1/4 cup olive oil

Seed Topping

1 tablespoon white sesame seeds

1 tablespoon poppy seeds

1/2 teaspoon cumin seeds

1 large egg white

Pinch of kosher salt or flaky or coarse sea salt

Line two rimmed baking sheets with parchment paper or silicone baking mats.

Combine the cornmeal, sorghum flour, rice flour, cornstarch, sugar, and salt in the bowl of a stand mixer fitted with the paddle attachment and blend for a few moments to mix. Form a well in the center of the flour mixture, pour in the warm water, and scatter the yeast over, stirring it in gently. Let sit until the yeast is frothy, about 5 minutes. Add the eggs and olive oil to the well and blend the wet and dry ingredients together at medium-low speed. When a cohesive dough forms, turn the dough out onto a work surface. The dough should feel a bit stickier than traditional bread dough, but if it's too sticky to work with, incorporate a bit more rice flour or cornstarch.

Cut the dough into 16 even pieces. Roll the dough portions out on the counter to form slender logs 9 to 10 inches long and about $^3/_4$ inch in diameter. Arrange the bread sticks on the prepared baking sheets about 2 inches apart. Note that this dough will be softer and more delicate than regular wheat-based dough you may be more familiar with; if necessary, you can always adjust the form or shape of the dough after it's on the baking sheet. Cover the baking sheets with plastic wrap (it is important to keep the dough from drying out) and set aside in a warm place until about doubled in bulk, 30 to 45 minutes.

Preheat the oven to 375°F. Set 2 oven racks at the centermost positions.

To make the topping, stir together the sesame seeds, poppy seeds, and cumin seeds in a small bowl. Beat the egg white with the salt in a small bowl until frothy. Very lightly brush the tops of the bread sticks with a bit of the egg white and sprinkle some of the seed mixture down the length of each, pressing gently to help them adhere. Bake until nicely puffed and lightly browned, about 20 minutes, switching the pans halfway through.

Transfer the bread sticks to a wire rack to cool, then arrange on a plate or in a basket for serving. These bread sticks will be best on the day they are made.

Crackers and Savory Cookies

Recipes in this chapter will, I hope, become some of your best friends, your go-to favorites for snack time. Crackers are generally easy-going snacks, something to grab by the handful to enjoy as is, to serve as the base for any number of toppings, such as cheeses, salami, tuna salad, you name it. Incorporating a range of flavors into the crackers themselves, from fresh herbs to citrus zest, only elevates their potential as stand-alone snacks. This chapter also includes savory twists on traditionally sweet cookies for a bit of playful and delicious fun.

The Best Crackers

There are a number of other cracker recipes in this book, and I think they're all great, of course. But I call this one "the best" because it's one of those recipes that should be in the standard repertoire of any snack-lover. The cracker has a really great texture: firm but not too hard, crisp but not too brittle. It holds up well to anything you may want to top it with, from cheese to chopped chicken livers. And it makes for a perfect blank slate for whatever embellishment suits your mood and what's on hand in your kitchen, whether you're adding fresh chopped herbs to the dough or sprinkling the crackers with a few different types of salts. For a seedy version of the crackers, consider topping them with some of the three-seed mixture used on the breadsticks on page 60.

I like to go with a slow rise for the yeast overnight in the refrigerator, rather than just setting the dough in a warm place and rising for an hour or so. The cool temperature slows down the yeast's activity, resulting in a more flavorful dough and one with a more distinctive texture. If time is of the essence though, you can simply let the dough rise in a warm place until doubled in bulk and proceed as noted. | **Makes 5 to 6 dozen crackers**

---

2 cups all-purpose flour, plus more as needed

1 teaspoon kosher salt or flaky or coarse sea salt, plus more for sprinkling

1/2 cup warm (105° to 110°F) water

2 teaspoons (1 envelope) active dry yeast

3 tablespoons olive oil

Finishing salt (see box)

Stir together the flour and salt in a medium bowl. Make a well in the center, pour the warm water into the well, and sprinkle the yeast over, stirring it in gently. Let sit until the yeast is frothy, about 5 minutes. Gently stir to start blending the wet and dry ingredients, drizzle the olive oil over, and continue stirring until a cohesive dough forms. Knead the dough on a lightly floured work surface for a few minutes until smooth and satiny. Return the dough to the bowl, cover well with plastic wrap, and refrigerate for 24 hours.

Preheat the oven to 375°F. Line 2 baking sheets with parchment paper or silicone baking mats.

Turn the dough out onto the counter, punch it down, and cut the dough into quarters. Use a pasta machine (see page 12) or rolling pin to roll the dough out into a rectangle about 1/16 inch thick, dusting lightly with flour as needed. Lightly brush the surface of the dough evenly with water, then sprinkle your choice of finishing salt over the surface. Use a dough docker (see page 9) or the tines of a fork to evenly prick the dough all over.

With the rolling blade of a pizza cutter or pastry wheel (plain or fluted), cut the dough into roughly $2^1/_2$ by $1^1/_2$-inch pieces (or whatever size and shape you would like). Arrange the dough pieces on the baking sheets; they can be snug but should not touch. Continue with the remaining dough portions. When 1 baking sheet is filled, bake until the crackers are lightly but evenly browned, 10 to 12 minutes. Some crackers around the edges of the baking sheet may be done sooner than those in the center; transfer them to a wire rack to cool and continue baking the rest for a minute or two longer.

Repeat until all the crackers have been formed and baked, filling one sheet while another is baking. Ideally the baking sheets should cool off before new crackers are added.

When all the crackers have cooled, arrange them in a basket or bowl for serving, or store in an airtight container for up to 1 week.

FINISHING SALT

If yours is like most kitchens today, you don't have just a standard box of table salt in the cupboard. Likely there's some kosher or sea salt somewhere, probably a specialty salt the likes of Murray River pink salt from Australia, alder-smoked salt from the Pacific Northwest, or those cool pyramid-shaped crystals of Maldon sea salt from England. These are all great candidates for a "finishing salt," which simply designates a salt that has a bit more prominent role in a dish, often sprinkled over the top just before it's served. The coarse or flaky grains of these salts will contribute distinct texture on the tongue, their individual flavors more easily highlighted.

This cracker recipe is an ideal means for trying out any and all of the different types of salts you have on hand. You might even consider mixing things up and topping a portion of the crackers with the different types. If, like me, you have some fancy salts that are quite coarsely grained, I recommend crushing them at least a bit before sprinkling over the crackers.

Poppy Seed Crackers

This is a versatile cracker that gains a bit of nutty character from the poppy seeds. As an alternative, consider using half poppy seeds and half sesame seeds, or all sesame seeds. The lively Feta-Lemon Spread on page 147 is a great topping for these crackers as is a simple slice of Cambozola cheese. | **Makes about 6 dozen crackers**

---

2 cups all-purpose flour, plus more if needed

$1/4$ cup poppy seeds

2 teaspoons baking powder

1 teaspoon kosher salt or flaky or coarse sea salt

$1/2$ cup water

$1/4$ cup olive oil

Preheat the oven to 375°F. Line 2 baking sheets with parchment paper or silicone baking mats.

Stir together the flour, poppy seeds, baking powder, and salt in a medium bowl and make a well in the center. Add the water and olive oil to the well and stir until a cohesive dough forms, kneading with your hands two or three times if needed to draw all the dough together. It's important to not overwork the dough, or it may become tough. Cut the dough into 4 even portions.

Use a pasta machine (see page 12) or rolling pin to roll 1 portion of the dough to a rectangle about $1/16$ inch thick, dusting lightly with flour as needed. With the rolling blade of a pizza cutter or pastry wheel (plain or fluted), cut the dough lengthwise into strips 2 to 3 inches wide, then across into 2-inch pieces. Arrange the dough pieces on a baking sheet; they can be snug but should not touch. When one of the baking sheets is filled, bake until the crackers are lightly browned and crisp, about 12 minutes.

Some crackers around the edges of the baking sheet may be done sooner than those in the center; transfer them to a wire rack to cool and continue baking the rest for a minute or two longer. Continue with the remaining dough portions until all the crackers have been formed and baked, filling one sheet while another is baking. Ideally the baking sheets should cool off before new crackers are added.

When all the crackers have cooled, arrange them in a basket or bowl for serving, or store in an airtight container for up to 1 week.

BAKING IN BATCHES

I found over the course of recipe testing for this book that I got the best, most consistent results when I baked thin items such as these crackers just 1 baking sheet at a time. Of course, that does draw out the overall oven time. If you prefer a more compact schedule, you can bake 2 baking sheets at once on the 2 centermost racks. Be sure to swap the sheets about halfway through baking and keep a good eye on their progress. Some crackers are likely to be browned and ready to come out before others, usually from the upper rack.

Almond–Olive Oil Crackers

These rich and flavorful crackers happen to be gluten-free, but there's no need to tell your gluten-loving guests anything about that. The texture is delightful and crisp, with a lightly nutty flavor. Note that not all baking powders are necessarily gluten-free, though many major brands are; be sure you're using a gluten-free baking powder if you'll be sharing these with any gluten-intolerant snackers. In fact, it's always best to confirm all ingredients used are noted as gluten-free on the packaging when it really counts.

There are commercial almond flours on the market, which are essentially very finely ground blanched almonds, though I prefer to grind them myself at home, lest I have yet one more ingredient to find a spot for on my already-overflowing kitchen shelves. Starting with slivered almonds, which you may find in bulk bins at the store, you're able to make just enough for this recipe. | **Makes about 5 dozen crackers**

- 1^1/$_2$ cups slivered blanched almonds (about 6^1/$_2$ ounces)
- ^{1}/$_2$ cup brown rice flour
- ^{1}/$_2$ cup cornstarch
- 1^1/$_2$ teaspoons baking powder
- 1^1/$_2$ teaspoons kosher salt or flaky or coarse sea salt
- 1 large egg white
- ^{1}/$_4$ cup water
- ^{1}/$_4$ cup olive oil

Preheat the oven to 400°F.

Pulse the almonds in a food processor until finely chopped. Add the brown rice flour and cornstarch and continue processing until the almonds are very finely ground to a near flourlike texture. (Working the flours with the almonds helps to keep the almonds from turning into a paste.) Add the baking powder and salt and pulse a few times to blend.

Transfer the almond mixture to a medium bowl. Beat the egg white until just lightly frothy in a small bowl, then add the water and stir until well blended. Add this to the almond mixture with the olive oil, stirring until a smooth and even dough is formed. Turn half of the dough out onto a large piece of parchment paper the size of your baking sheet and use your fingers to spread it out into a relatively even rectangle, about 6 by 8 inches. Top the dough with another piece of parchment paper and roll the dough out to a rectangle about ^{3}/$_8$ inch thick. Remove and save the top piece of parchment paper.

Use the rolling blade of a pizza cutter or pastry wheel (plain or fluted) to cut the dough into roughly 2-inch squares. Transfer the dough—still on the sheet of parchment paper—to a baking sheet and bake until lightly but evenly browned and crisp, 10 to 12 minutes. Some crackers around the edges of the baking sheet may be done sooner than those in the center; transfer them to a wire rack to cool and continue baking the rest for a minute or two longer. For these crackers in particular, pale crackers will have a dull flavor; better a touch overcooked than undercooked.

While the first sheet is baking, roll out and cut the remaining dough in the same fashion. Bake the second sheet after the first sheet is done.

When all of the crackers have cooled, arrange them in a basket or bowl for serving, or store in an airtight container for up to 2 days.

THE SHAPE OF THINGS

The beauty of making your own crackers at home is that once the dough has been rolled out, there's almost no limit to the shapes the final cracker can take. I do cut out the rye crackers on page 76 with a round cutter, but for most of the recipes in this book I lean more toward rectangular shapes. This is for the simple reason that the quick swipe of a rolling pastry cutter makes efficient work of cutting the dough, no individual forms to be cut, and no trim to discard or reshape to roll again. But the final shape is up to you: smaller squares, long slender fingers, diamond shapes, trapezoids.

Oh, and don't worry about all the crackers having exactly the same dimensions. No matter how hard I try, I can rarely roll the dough out to

a perfectly formed rectangle, so inevitably the corners are more rounded than square and the edges might bulge a bit. If you want fastidiously consistent crackers, go ahead and trim the sides before cutting the crackers. Otherwise, take comfort in the fact that "rustic" is a very chic look for crackers.

Of course, you're not obliged to cut the dough into individual crackers at all. Instead, individual portions of rolled-out dough can be baked in their whole, rectangular form. Simply transfer as is to the baking sheet and bake (it will likely require a few extra minutes in the oven). You can then serve the big crackers as is on a plate or in a long slender basket and have your guests break off their own portions, or break them into smaller pieces before serving.

Rosemary Cornmeal Crackers

Cooking fresh rosemary leaves in butter accomplishes two delicious goals for these crackers: The rosemary gets lightly crisped and the butter takes on the flavor and aroma of the herb. The butter will also "brown" a bit as well, developing an added nutty character that complements the cornmeal beautifully. | **Makes about 5 dozen crackers**

1/2 cup unsalted butter

2 tablespoons fresh rosemary leaves, plucked from the stem

1 1/4 cups all-purpose flour, plus more if needed

3/4 cup fine yellow cornmeal

1 teaspoon kosher salt or flaky or coarse sea salt, plus more for sprinkling

1/2 cup whole milk

Preheat the oven to 350°F. Line 2 baking sheets with parchment paper or silicone baking mats.

Melt the butter in a small skillet over medium heat. Add the rosemary and cook, stirring occasionally with a fork, until the rosemary is lightly crisped and aromatic but not browned, 2 to 3 minutes. Use the fork to lift out the rosemary (allowing excess butter to drip back into the skillet) and scatter it on a small plate. Let cool, then press on the leaves with the back of the fork to evenly crush them. Reserve the melted butter and the rosemary.

Combine the flour, cornmeal, and salt in a medium bowl and stir well to blend, then make a well in the center. Add the milk, rosemary, and 1/4 cup of the reserved melted butter to the well and stir just until a cohesive dough forms, kneading with your hands two or three times if needed to draw the dough together. It's important to avoid overworking the dough, or it may become tough. Cut the dough into 4 even portions.

Use a pasta machine (see page 12) or rolling pin to roll 1 portion of the dough out to a rectangle about 1/16 inch thick, dusting lightly with flour as needed. Lightly brush the surface with some of the reserved melted butter and sprinkle with salt. With the rolling blade of a pizza cutter or pastry wheel (plain or fluted), cut the dough lengthwise in half or thirds, then across into 2-inch pieces. Arrange the pieces on the prepared baking sheets; they can be snug but not touching. When 1 baking sheet is filled, bake until the crackers are lightly browned and crisp, 12 to 15 minutes. Some crackers around the edges of the baking sheet may be done sooner than those in the center; transfer them to a wire rack to cool and continue baking the rest for a minute or two longer. Continue with the remaining dough portions until all the crackers have been formed and baked, filling 1 sheet while another is baking. Ideally the baking sheets should cool off before new crackers are added.

When all the crackers have cooled, arrange them in a basket or bowl for serving, or store in an airtight container for up to 4 days.

Herbes de Provence Crackers

These butter-enriched crackers have a lovely crunch and great texture. I think fresh goat cheese is a particularly good choice to partner with them, the herbal flavor of the crackers an ideal complement to the mild, slightly tangy cheese. If you've made the Five-Spice Duck Skin (page 101) and have some duck fat on hand, consider replacing the melted butter here with melted duck fat. The resulting crackers are a bit more delicate in texture, but the flavor sure is amazing. | **Makes about 5 dozen crackers**

---

2 cups all-purpose flour

1^1/$_2$ teaspoons dried herbes de Provence

^{3}/$_4$ teaspoon kosher salt or flaky or coarse sea salt, plus more for sprinkling

A few grindings black pepper

^{1}/$_4$ cup unsalted butter, melted, plus more for brushing

^{1}/$_2$ cup water

Put the flour in a medium bowl. Crush the herbes de Provence in a small mortar and pestle or rub it between your palms and add the herbs to the flour with the salt and pepper. Stir to mix, then add the butter and stir well to blend until the mixture has the texture of coarse cornmeal. Add the water and stir just until a cohesive dough forms, kneading with your hands two or three times if needed to draw all the dough together. It's important to avoid overworking the dough, or it may become tough. Cut the dough into 4 even portions.

Preheat the oven to 375°F. Line 2 baking sheets with parchment paper or silicone baking mats.

Use a pasta machine (see page 12) or rolling pin to roll out 1 portion of the dough to a rect-angle about ^{1}/$_{16}$ inch thick, dusting lightly with flour as needed. Brush the surface lightly with melted butter and sprinkle with salt. Use a dough docker (see page 9) or the tines of a fork to evenly prick the dough all over. With the rolling blade of a pizza cutter or pastry wheel (plain or fluted), cut the dough in half lengthwise, then across into strips about 1^1/$_2$ inches wide. Arrange the dough pieces on a baking sheet; they can be snug but should not touch. When 1 baking sheet is filled, bake until the crackers are just lightly browned and crisp, 12 to 15 minutes. Some crackers around the edges of the baking sheet may be done sooner than those in the center; transfer them to a wire rack to cool and bake the rest for a minute or two longer. Continue with the remaining dough portions until all the crackers have been formed and baked, filling one sheet while another is baking. Ideally the baking sheets should cool off before new crackers are added.

When all the crackers have cooled, arrange them in a basket or bowl for serving, or store in an airtight container for up to 1 week.

Fennel *and* Orange Crackers

The aromatic character of fennel and orange marry well in this whole wheat cracker. It makes a great option to serve with a cheese platter for cocktail nibbles or an after-dinner savory alternative to dessert. | **Makes about 5 dozen crackers**

1/2 cup whole milk

6 tablespoons unsalted butter, cut into pieces

1 1/2 cups all-purpose flour, plus more if needed

3/4 cup whole wheat flour

1 tablespoon finely grated orange zest

2 teaspoons fennel seeds, freshly ground

3/4 teaspoon kosher salt or flaky or coarse sea salt

1 large egg, well beaten

Melted unsalted butter, for brushing

Orange salt (see box), flaky or coarse sea salt, or kosher salt, for finishing

Combine the milk and butter in a small saucepan and warm gently over medium-low heat until the butter is melted. Set aside to cool to room temperature.

Stir together the all-purpose flour, whole wheat flour, orange zest, fennel, and salt in a medium bowl. Make a well in the center of the dry ingredients and add the cooled milk/butter mixture and beaten egg to the well. Stir until a cohesive dough forms, adding a bit more all-purpose flour, if needed. Knead the dough with your hands two or three times if needed to draw all the dough together. Cut the dough into 4 even portions.

Preheat the oven to 350°F. Line 2 baking sheets with parchment paper or silicone baking mats.

Use a pasta machine (see page 12) or rolling pin to roll 1 portion of dough to a rectangle about 1/16 inch thick, dusting lightly with flour as needed. Brush the surface with a thin layer of melted butter and sprinkle lightly with the salt. Use a dough docker (see page 9) or the tines of a fork to evenly prick the dough all over.

With the rolling blade of a pizza cutter or pastry wheel (plain or fluted), cut the dough lengthwise in halves or thirds, then across into 2-inch pieces. Arrange the dough pieces on a baking sheet; they can be snug but should not touch. When 1 baking sheet is filled, bake until the crackers are lightly but evenly browned, 15 to 17 minutes. Some crackers around the edges of the baking sheet may be done sooner than those in the center; transfer them to a wire rack to cool and continue baking the rest for a minute or two longer. Continue with the remaining dough portions until all the crackers have been formed and baked, filling one sheet while another is baking. Ideally the baking sheets should cool off before new crackers are added.

When all the crackers have cooled, arrange them in a basket or bowl for serving, or store in an airtight container for up to 1 week.

CITRUS SALT

There are a lot of interesting types of salts on the market these days, but it's easy to create some distinctive salt combinations at home, too. One of my favorites is as simple as rubbing together finely grated citrus zest with a flaky sea salt or kosher salt. The rough edges of the salt crystals rubbing against the zest strips help release the essential oils from the zest, quickly creating an aromatic salt. I just combine the two in a small bowl and grab portions at a time to rub between my fingers for a few seconds, the whole process taking a minute or so total. About $1/2$ teaspoon zest per tablespoon of salt is a good proportion to use. The flavor and aroma will be best if you do this shortly before using the salt. If you'd like a more finely textured result, combine the salt and zest in a mini food processor and pulse until well blended.

Cumin Lentil Crackers

Lentils and chickpea flour serve as the base for this gluten-free cracker, embellished with the warm, aromatic character of ground cumin. The dough is a bit more delicate than others that have some "give" thanks to the natural gluten in wheat flours; it may split a bit as you roll it out, but just press with your fingers to seal any gaps. These crackers are tasty dipped into the Cucumber and Radish Tzatziki (page 144), or topped with the Artichoke–Roasted Garlic Spread (page 149).

I prefer to use red lentils for this recipe, for their lighter color and their natural tendency to become quite soft when cooked. Brown lentils can be used instead, they'll need about 5 minutes longer cooking time and you may want to add an extra tablespoon of water to help make a smooth puree. Those lovely French green lentils are best saved for another recipe. | **Makes about 5 dozen crackers**

1/3 cup red lentils

1 bay leaf, preferably fresh

1 clove garlic, lightly crushed

1/2 teaspoon kosher salt or flaky or coarse sea salt, plus more for lentils

3 tablespoons olive oil

1 tablespoon water, plus more if needed

1/2 cup chickpea flour, plus more for rolling out dough

1/4 cup sweet (white) rice flour

1 1/2 teaspoons ground cumin

Preheat the oven to 350°F. Line 2 baking sheets with parchment paper or silicone baking mats.

Put the lentils, bay leaf, and garlic clove in a small saucepan with a pinch of salt and add cold water to cover by 2 inches. Bring the water to a boil over medium-high heat, then reduce the heat to medium and simmer until the lentils are very tender, about 15 minutes.

The water should not boil; reduce the heat to medium-low if needed. Drain the lentils and discard the bay leaf and garlic clove. Let the lentils cool, then puree them in a food processor (a mini if you have one, see page 10) with the olive oil and water until smooth.

Transfer the lentil puree to a bowl and stir in the chickpea flour, rice flour, cumin, and salt. Stir to form a cohesive dough that's not crumbly; drizzle in a bit more water, if needed. Form the dough into a ball on the counter and cut it into 4 even portions.

On a work surface lightly dusted with chickpea flour, roll 1 portion of dough to a roughly 7-inch square about 1/16 inch thick. Use the rolling blade of a pizza cutter or pastry wheel (plain or fluted) to cut the square in quarters each direction, making 16 squares. Arrange the dough pieces on a baking sheet;

they can be snug but should not touch. When 1 baking sheet is filled, bake until the crackers are lightly but evenly browned, 15 to 17 minutes. Some crackers around the edges of the baking sheet may be done sooner than those in the center; transfer them to a wire rack to cool and continue baking the rest for a minute or two longer. Continue with the remaining dough portions until all the crackers have been formed and baked, filling 1 sheet while another is baking. Ideally the baking sheets should cool off before new crackers are added.

When all the crackers have cooled, arrange them in a basket or bowl for serving, or store in an airtight container for up to 1 week.

CRACKER HISTORY

Crackers may be somewhat upscale snacks today, but they evolved from a foundation that was far from gastronomic. Simple dry biscuits and flatbreads have been made in many parts of the world for countless generations. In the United States, it was in the late nineteenth century that a forerunner to today's crackers, known as pilot bread, hardtack, or ship's bread, was in wide production. These thin, dry, firm foods were made from little more than flour and water to promise a maximum of shelf life and were packed along as sustenance for long sea journeys or extensive westward explorations. (My dad, the retired Navy guy, also packed them along on backpacking trips when I was a kid; lunch was often pilot bread with peanut butter on top.)

Over the years, those spartan recipes changed to improve flavor and texture—incorporating fat and seasonings, for starters—which gave us the advent of the soda cracker and other more generally enjoyable crackers in the mid to late 1800s. Since then the floodgates have opened, and we have countless crackers to choose from, from the still-classic water cracker to wasabi rice crackers for a change of pace.

Rye Crackers *with Caraway*

This is a full-flavored cracker that really stands alone well as a snack, with layers of savory character from the rye flour and caraway seeds. However, the crackers can also serve as an ideal vehicle for a spread such as the Deviled Ham with Pickled Peppers (page 150) or extra-sharp cheddar cheese. | **Makes 5 to 6 dozen crackers**

---

1 1/4 cups dark rye flour

3/4 cup all-purpose flour

1 tablespoon baking powder

1 teaspoon kosher salt or flaky or coarse sea salt, plus more for sprinkling

3/4 cup buttermilk

3 tablespoons olive oil

2 teaspoons caraway seeds

Preheat the oven to 350°F. Line 2 baking sheets with parchment paper or silicone baking mats.

Stir together the rye flour, all-purpose flour, baking powder, and salt in a medium bowl. Make a well in the center and add the buttermilk and olive oil to the well. Stir the ingredients together until a cohesive dough forms, kneading with your hands two or three times if needed to draw all the dough together. It's important to avoid overworking the dough, or it may become tough.

Cut the dough into 2 even portions, setting 1 piece aside under a kitchen towel to avoid drying out. Roll the dough out on a lightly floured work surface to a 12- to 14-inch circle, about 1/16 inch thick. Use a dough docker (see page 9) or the tines of a fork to evenly prick the dough all over.

With a round cookie cutter (2 to 2 1/4 inches), cut circles from the dough, arranging them on the prepared baking sheets about 1/2 inch apart. Lightly brush the surface of each round with a bit of water and sprinkle lightly with caraway seeds and salt, pressing gently to help them adhere to the dough. Arrange the dough pieces on a baking sheet; they can be snug but should not touch.

When one of the baking sheets is filled, bake until lightly browned and crisp, 15 to 17 minutes. Some crackers around the edges of the baking sheet may be done sooner than those in the center; transfer them to a wire rack to cool and continue baking the rest for a minute or two longer. Continue forming and baking the remaining crackers to fill the other baking sheet, gently gathering the trim from each half just once to roll out again to 1/16 inch thick. (The dough is likely to become tough if reformed and rerolled too many times.)

When all the crackers have cooled, arrange them in a basket or bowl for serving, or store in an airtight container for up to 1 week.

Savory Hazelnut-Fig Shortbread

Pure and simple shortbread is a favorite cookie of mine, so it was a fun leap from there to come up with a savory variation. Hazelnuts and dried figs are one of those delightful flavor matches, lovely in salads or for stuffing a pork loin. Here they pair up beautifully in a snack that's great on its own. Or consider topping the shortbreads with Stilton or an aged cheddar cheese, perhaps with a dab of fig compote.

You can chop the hazelnuts in a food processor if you like; but if doing so, be sure to add $1/4$ cup of the flour to whirl with the nuts. This will help prevent accidentally going from finely chopped hazelnuts to hazelnut butter. The figs are too soft to chop well in the machine; best to take care of that task by hand. | **Makes 4 to 5 dozen shortbreads**

$3/4$ cup unsalted butter, at room temperature

$1/2$ cup finely chopped toasted hazelnuts

2 cups all-purpose flour

$1/2$ cup finely chopped dried figs

$1^1/2$ teaspoons kosher salt or flaky or coarse sea salt

$1/4$ teaspoon finely grated lemon zest

Cream together the butter and hazelnuts in the bowl of a stand mixer fitted with the paddle attachment until evenly blended and smooth, scraping down the sides once or twice. Stir together the flour, figs, salt, and lemon zest in a small bowl. With the mixer at low speed, gradually add the flour mixture, working just until it is evenly incorporated and the dough begins to pull together.

Transfer the dough to a 24-inch piece of parchment paper or waxed paper and press the dough out to a strip about 16 inches long down the center of the paper. Fold the long edges of the paper up over the dough and form the dough into a log about $1^1/2$ inches in diameter. Twist the ends of the paper to seal the log and refrigerate the dough for at least 30 minutes, or overnight.

Preheat the oven to 350°F. Line 2 baking sheets with parchment paper or silicone baking mats. Set 2 oven racks at the 2 centermost positions.

Unwrap the dough log and use a sharp, thin-bladed knife to cut across into $1/4$-inch slices. Arrange the slices on the baking sheets, about $1/2$ inch apart. Bake until lightly browned and firm to the touch, 15 to 17 minutes, switching the pans about halfway through.

Let cool for a few minutes on the baking sheet, then transfer the shortbread to a wire rack to cool completely. When all the crackers have cooled, arrange them in a basket or bowl for serving, or store the shortbread in an airtight container for up to 3 days.

Taralli

This Italian savory snack looks like a mini bagel but is firm like a hard pretzel, with a flaky texture all its own—an ideal treat to enjoy with a glass of wine or cocktail. Different types of *taralli* are made in different regions of Italy. The kind I fell in love with on a recent trip are from the Puglia region, made with white wine and olive oil. *Taralli* became a favorite travel snack for train-ride picnics and long stints in the rental car. There are many possible flavor variations— we sampled onion (see box), fennel, and garlic on our trip. | **Makes 32 *taralli***

---

2 cups all-purpose flour

1 1/2 teaspoons kosher salt or flaky or coarse sea salt

1/2 cup dry white wine

1/2 cup olive oil

Stir together the flour and salt in a bowl. Add the wine and olive oil and stir until a cohesive dough forms. Shape into a ball, cover the bowl with a towel, and let sit for 1 hour to allow the flour to absorb moisture from the liquids.

Turn the dough out onto the counter and cut it into 8 even portions. Roll 1 portion of the dough into a rope about 20 inches long and 1/2 inch in diameter. Cut the dough rope across into 5-inch pieces and form each piece into a circle, gently pinching at the ends to seal. Set the formed dough on a baking sheet while rolling and forming the remaining dough.

Preheat the oven to 350°F. Line a rimmed baking sheet with parchment paper or a silicone baking mat.

Bring a large pan of salted water to a boil over medium-high heat. Gently add 6 or 7 of the *taralli* to the water and simmer until they rise to the surface, about 2 minutes. Scoop them out with a slotted spoon, drain for a moment over the pan, and arrange them on the prepared baking sheet. They won't expand much while baking, so can be close together but should not be touching. Repeat with the remaining *taralli*, allowing the water to reheat between batches as needed. Bake the *taralli* until lightly browned and crisp, about 45 minutes. Transfer the *taralli* to a wire rack to cool.

When all the *taralli* have cooled, arrange them in a basket or bowl for serving, or store them in an airtight container for up to 5 days.

ONION TARALLI

Combine 1/4 cup of the olive oil and 1/2 cup finely chopped onion in a small saucepan. Cook over medium-low heat until the onion is quite tender, lightly browned, and aromatic, 25 to 30 minutes. Set aside to cool, then add the onion-oil mixture to the flour with the remaining 1/4 cup of olive oil and the wine. Continue as directed. The onion may contribute just enough extra moisture to the dough that you need to use a bit more flour; add just enough so that the dough is not sticky.

Modern Melba

This is, admittedly, a bit of a leap from the original Melba toast. The great chef Auguste Escoffier is credited as creator of that humble cracker, which is little more than thin slices of bread toasted in the oven. He was inspired by the ailing Dame Nellie Melba, an Australian opera star, who needed a delicate snack while feeling under the weather. (She was the chef's muse, too, for the eponymous peach Melba dessert, created on a more celebratory occasion, to be sure.)

Melba goes modern here. I adapted the original's versatile size and characteristic crunch with ingredients that add flavor and texture, creating an ideal foundation for any number of spreads, toppings, and dips. These toasts are particularly well suited to serve with a cheese tray, whether as a before-dinner snack or savory "dessert" course. The Roasted Pepper and Walnut Spread (page 146) is delicious with these crackers as well. | **Makes about 4 dozen toasts**

1^1/$_4$ cups whole milk

3 tablespoons honey

1 cup all-purpose flour, plus more if needed

1 cup whole wheat flour

^{1}/$_2$ cup dark rye flour

^{1}/$_2$ cup toasted pumpkin seeds

^{1}/$_4$ cup white sesame seeds or poppy seeds

^{1}/$_4$ cup finely chopped toasted hazelnuts or walnuts

2 tablespoons finely chopped fresh rosemary

2 teaspoons baking powder

1 teaspoon kosher salt or flaky or coarse sea salt

Preheat the oven to 375°F. Generously butter an 8- or 9-inch square cake pan.

In a small saucepan, combine the milk and honey and warm over medium-low heat just until the honey is melted, stirring occasionally. Set aside.

Combine the all-purpose flour, whole-wheat flour, rye flour, pumpkin seeds, sesame seeds, hazelnuts, rosemary, baking powder, and salt in a large bowl. Add the warm milk and stir just until a cohesive dough forms. The dough will be on the sticky side; if it's too sticky to easily manage, stir in another tablespoon or two of all-purpose flour. Spoon the dough into the prepared baking pan, spreading it out evenly.

Bake the bread until a toothpick inserted in the center comes out clean, 20 to 25 minutes. Let cool slightly in the pan, then turn the bread out onto a wire rack to cool completely. Reduce the oven temperature to 300°F.

Cut the bread in half crosswise, then cut each half across into slices about ^{1}/$_8$ inch thick. (Freezing the bread for about 30 minutes will make it easier to cut even slices.) Arrange the slices on 2 rimmed baking sheets; they can be snug but avoid overlapping.

Toast the bread in the oven for 15 minutes, then flip the bread slices over and return the pans to the same racks. Toast for 15 minutes longer, then switch the pans onto opposite racks. Toast for another 15 minutes, and once again flip the bread slices, returning the pans to the same racks. Toast for 10 to 15 minutes longer, until the slices are nicely crisped and lightly browned. You may find that some slices are ready to be removed earlier, while others need extra time.

Let the toasts cool completely on the baking sheets, then transfer to a basket or a bowl for serving, or store in an airtight container for up to 1 week.

Blue Cheese Straws

"Cheese straw" is something of a catch-all term for any number of types of pastry embellished with savory cheese. It can be as simple as strips of puff pastry topped with grated cheese, but I love this type that's based on an easy homemade, buttery dough. Dry crumbly types of blue cheese, such as Gorgonzola or Roquefort, will be better here than a creamy Cambozola.
| **Makes about 42 cheese straws**

---

1 cup finely crumbled blue cheese (about 4 ounces)

3/4 cup unsalted butter, at room temperature

2 cups all-purpose flour

1/2 teaspoon kosher salt or flaky or coarse sea salt

1/4 teaspoon freshly ground black pepper

Cream together the cheese and butter in the bowl of a stand mixer fitted with the paddle attachment until evenly blended and smooth, scraping down the sides once or twice. Stir together the flour, salt, and pepper in a small bowl. With the mixer at low speed, gradually add the flour, working just until it is evenly incorporated and the dough begins to pull together. Form the dough into a roughly 6-inch square, wrap in plastic, and refrigerate to firm slightly, about 30 minutes. (The dough can be made further in advance, up to a day, but it becomes quite hard and will need to sit at room temperature for about 1 hour to soften enough to roll out.)

Preheat the oven to 375°F. Line 2 rimmed baking sheets with parchment paper or silicone baking mats. Set 2 oven racks at the center-most positions.

Working on a lightly floured surface, roll the dough out to a rectangle about 12 inches by 14 inches. The dough should be about 1/4 inch thick. Use the rolling blade of a pizza cutter or pastry wheel (plain or fluted) to cut the dough into pieces about 4 inches long and 1 inch wide. Set the pieces on the baking sheets, about 1/2 inch apart.

Bake until lightly browned and firm, 15 to 17 minutes, switching the pans about halfway through. Let the cheese straws cool on the baking sheets for a few minutes, then transfer them to a wire rack to cool completely.

When all the cheese straws have cooled, arrange them in a basket or bowl for serving, or store the cheese straws in an airtight container for up to 5 days.

Spicy Peanut Butter Cookies *with Dukka*

These look like yummy, traditionally sweet peanut butter cookies—so it's up to you whether you warn your friends about the savory, spice-enhanced flavor before they bite in! Dukka, a Middle Eastern nut-based seasoning mix, makes a flavorful accent of nutty texture to coat the cookies. The dukka can be made up to 1 week ahead and stored in an airtight container. | **Makes about 3 dozen cookies**

Peanut Dukka

    3 tablespoons white sesame seeds

1 1/2 teaspoons cumin seeds

    1 teaspoon coriander seeds

3/4 cup roasted peanuts

    1 teaspoon sweet Hungarian paprika

1/2 teaspoon kosher salt or flaky or coarse
        sea salt

    1 cup all-purpose flour

    1 teaspoon baking powder

    1 teaspoon kosher salt or flaky or coarse
        sea salt

1/2 to 1 teaspoon red pepper flakes

1 1/2 cups creamy natural peanut butter, at room
        temperature

1/4 cup unsalted butter, at room temperature

    2 tablespoons packed light brown sugar

    2 large eggs

For the dukka, combine the sesame seeds, cumin seeds, and coriander seeds in a small dry skillet and toast over medium heat until the sesame seeds are just lightly browned and the other seeds are aromatic, 2 to 3 minutes. Transfer to a food processor, let cool for a minute or two, then pulse a few times to partly grind the seeds. Add the peanuts and pulse until they are finely chopped and well blended with the seeds (avoid over-processing or the mixture may turn to a paste). Add the paprika and salt and pulse a few times to blend. Transfer to a shallow bowl and set aside.

Preheat the oven to 350°F. Line 2 baking sheets with parchment paper or silicone baking mats. Set 2 oven racks at the centermost positions.

Stir together the flour, baking powder, salt, and pepper flakes in a medium bowl.

Stir together the peanut butter, butter, and brown sugar in a large bowl until well blended. Stir in the eggs, one at a time, beating well after each addition. Add half of the flour and stir until incorporated, then stir in the rest to form a smooth dough. Pinch off some dough and roll it between your palms into a ball about 1 1/4 inches in diameter. Roll the ball in the dukka to evenly but lightly coat it and set it on the baking sheet. Repeat with the rest of the dough, arranging the balls about 2 inches apart. Use the bottom of a glass to flatten the balls to about 2 inches in diameter, twisting the glass a bit as you lift it up to help avoid sticking. Bake the cookies until firm to the touch, about 20 minutes, switching the pans halfway through. Let cool for a few minutes on the baking sheets, then transfer to a wire rack.

Arrange the cookies on a platter for serving, or store in an airtight container for up to 3 days.

Parmesan Thumbprint Cookies
with Tomato–Tart Cherry Jam

This harkens to those beloved jam-filled cookies that have been favorites in cookies jars for generations. This savory twist embellishes the dough with Parmesan cheese, the jam in question made with tomato and tart cherries. The jam recipe makes more than is needed for this batch of cookies, but it's not practical to make in smaller quantities. Extra will keep well in an airtight container in the refrigerator for up to 2 weeks. Spread it on turkey or ham sandwiches, slather it on chicken breasts before baking, or serve as an accompaniment to cheese. You can use dried cranberries in place of the dried tart cherries, if you like.

For a short-cut version, you could nix making the jam here and simply use prepared plum or fig jam, or another minimally sweet jam. | **Makes 2 dozen cookies**

Tomato–Tart Cherry Jam

- 1 tablespoon olive oil
- 3 tablespoons minced shallot or onion
- 1 cup finely chopped seeded tomato (see box, page 86)
- 1/2 cup dried tart cherries
- 1/4 cup water, plus more if needed
- 3/4 teaspoon minced fresh thyme, or 1/4 teaspoon dried thyme
- 1/2 teaspoon kosher salt or flaky or coarse sea salt

- 13/4 cups all-purpose flour
- 3/4 cup finely grated Parmesan cheese
- 1/2 cup unsalted butter, at room temperature
- 1/2 cup cream cheese, at room temperature
- 1/4 teaspoon kosher salt or flaky or coarse sea salt

To make the jam, heat the olive oil in a small saucepan over medium heat. Add the shallot and cook, stirring often, until tender and aromatic but not browned, 2 to 3 minutes. Stir in the tomato, dried cherries, water, thyme, and salt and continue cooking until the cherries are plumped and the tomatoes are soft, about 10 minutes, stirring occasionally. Let cool, then puree the jam in the food processor, adding a bit more water as needed to achieve a texture a bit thinner than applesauce. Set aside.

Preheat the oven to 350°F. Line a rimmed baking sheet with parchment paper or a silicone baking mat.

Combine the flour and Parmesan cheese in a food processor and pulse until the cheese is finely ground and well blended with the flour.

---

continued on next page

Add the butter and cream cheese and pulse just until a cohesive dough forms, scraping down the sides as needed; avoid overmixing.

Form the dough into 24 balls about $1^1/4$ inches in diameter and set them on the baking sheet about 1 inch apart. Press your thumb into the center of each ball to make an indentation (it's normal for the edges to crack a bit, butyou can gently pinch together any particularly large cracks). Fill each indentation with some of the jam, about $^1/2$ teaspoon each.

Bake the cookies until firm and nicely browned around the edges, 30 to 35 minutes. Because this dough is a bit dense, be sure the cookies are thoroughly cooked, beyond just a light golden brown. If you pull them out too soon they may still be a bit underdone in the center. You can always snag one from the tray and break it in two to check—a snack for the cook.

Let cool slightly on the baking sheets, then transfer to a wire rack to cool completely. Arrange the cookies on a platter for serving, or store in an airtight container for up to 2 days.

SEEDING TOMATOES

In most recipes for which I'm using fresh tomatoes, I don't bother with seeding them before using. But in this case, I do prefer to use just the firmer tomato flesh, discarding the seeds before chopping the tomato. In this concentrated jam-like mixture, omitting the seeds—which hold a lot of moisture in the membrane that surrounds them—results in a smoother, more consistent texture in the end.

To remove the seeds, I halve the tomato across the middle (rather than from end-to-end) and simply use my fingers to scoop out the seeds from the separate cavities in which they're nestled.

Dark Chocolate Oat Cookies

This recipe is inspired by a cookie I fell in love with at Teaism in Washington, DC. That big, sweet treat is dotted with pieces of chocolate in a rich dough specked with oats and accented with salt. My interpretation of the theme takes things to the savory side, with some added nutty-crunchy character coming from cocoa nibs. This is ideal to accompany an afternoon pick-me-up cup of coffee or tea. Look for cocoa nibs—small pieces of roasted cocoa bean—with baking goods in well-stocked grocery stores, at specialty chocolate shops, or from online resources (see page 154). When forming the dough into a log for chilling, feel free to stray from the traditional rounded shapes, if you like. Pressing it on four sides will create square-shaped cookies when sliced. | **Makes about 4 dozen cookies**

---

1 cup old-fashioned rolled oats

3/4 cup all-purpose flour

1/2 cup unsweetened cocoa powder

2 teaspoons kosher salt or flaky or coarse sea salt

1/2 cup unsalted butter, at room temperature

1/4 cup plus 2 teaspoons packed light brown sugar

1 large egg

1/4 cup cocoa nibs (optional)

Pulse 1/2 cup of the oats in a food processor (a mini if you have one, see page 10) to finely grind them. Combine the ground oats with the remaining oats, flour, cocoa powder, and 1 teaspoon of the salt in a medium bowl and stir to mix.

Cream the butter and 1/4 cup of the brown sugar in the bowl of a stand mixer fitted with the paddle attachment. Beat in the egg, scraping down the sides as needed. With the mixer at low speed, slowly add the oat mixture, followed by the cocoa nibs. Transfer the dough to an 18-inch piece of parchment or waxed paper and press the dough out to a strip about 12 inches long down the center of the paper. Fold the long edges of the paper up over the dough and form the dough into a log about 1 1/2 inches in diameter. Twist the ends of the paper to seal and refrigerate for at least 30 minutes, or overnight.

Preheat the oven to 350°F. Line 2 baking sheets with parchment paper or silicone baking mats. Set 2 oven racks at the centermost positions.

Stir together the remaining 2 teaspoons of brown sugar and 1 teaspoon of salt in a small bowl. Unwrap the dough and use a sharp, thin-bladed knife to cut across the log into 1/4-inch slices. Arrange on the baking sheet, about 1/2 inch apart, and sprinkle with the sugar-salt mixture. Bake until firm to the touch, about 15 minutes, switching the pans halfway through.

Let cool for a few minutes on the baking sheet, then transfer to a wire rack.

Arrange the cookies on a platter for serving, or store them in an airtight container for up to 3 days.

Meat and Seafood

Just because the subject is "snacks" doesn't mean that meats and seafood can't come to the party, too. There are a lot of ways to transform fish and shellfish, beef, and poultry into small perfectly snackable bites. This chapter's a fun example of just how much potential variety there is in the realm of snacks, well beyond the beloved foundation of crackers, chips, and popcorn. And when you feel like breaking the dinner-party mold and sharing a snack-heavy spread with your friends, there are some great options here to help create a satisfying grazing meal.

Crisp Shrimp with Shichimi Togarashi | 90

Half Shell Oysters with Grapefruit-Campari Granita | 92

Smoked Salmon Rillettes | 93

Smoked Salmon with Ginger and Black Pepper | 94

Pickled Trout with Horseradish Sauce | 97

Salt Cod and Potato Puffs | 99

Sesame Chicken Bites | 100

Five-Spice Duck Skin | 101

Duck Jerky | 102

Salami Chips with Grainy Mustard Dip | 104

Deviled Bacon | 106

Crisp Beef with Lemongrass | 107

Crisp Shrimp *with Shichimi Togarashi*

Ahhh, fried shrimp. One of the classic go-to snacks for bar patrons everywhere. This version is a light and flavorful take, with a simple coating of rice flour rather than a heavy batter. And the shrimp are seasoned with one of my favorite spices, *shichimi togarashi*, a Japanese pepper blend that typically includes red pepper flakes, dried orange zest, sesame seeds, and dried seaweed among other seasonings. I love it sprinkled over a piece of salmon or halibut that's simply grilled or baked, or stirred into plain steamed rice. Wonderful. | **Makes 4 to 6 servings**

---

1 teaspoon shichimi togarashi

1 teaspoon kosher salt or flaky or coarse sea salt

1 pound large (16/20) shrimp, peeled

1/2 cup sweet (white) rice flour

Vegetable oil, for frying

Stir together the *shichimi togarashi* and salt in a small bowl.

Use a small sharp knife to slit each shrimp along its back, removing any dark vein from the shrimp. Continue to slice through the shrimp from the back, halving each completely.

Put the shrimp in a medium bowl and sprinkle half of the seasoned salt over, tossing to mix. Add the rice flour and toss to evenly coat the shrimp.

Pour about 2 inches of oil in a large heavy saucepan (the oil should not come more than halfway up the sides of the pan). Bring to 375°F over medium heat. Add 6 to 8 pieces of shrimp to the oil at a time, cooking until crisped and lightly browned, 1 to 2 minutes. Lift the shrimp out with a slotted spoon and transfer to paper towels to drain. Sprinkle some of the remaining seasoned salt over them. Continue cooking and seasoning the shrimp in batches, allowing the oil to reheat between batches as needed.

Transfer the crisp shrimp to a bowl and serve. They are best enjoyed shortly after cooking.

Half Shell Oysters *with* Grapefruit-Campari Granita

Oysters are nature's perfect salty snack. But for those of us who don't mind a little gilding of the lily, this granita is a simple way to dress up the bivalves. The citrusy flavor—with the touch of bitterness from the Campari—and icy texture beautifully contrast the briny richness of the oysters. I love Kusshi and Kumamoto oysters, but choose whatever's freshest in your local seafood shop.

The granita recipe makes about 3½ cups, far more than is needed for a couple dozen oysters, plenty for at least quadruple that. The extra will keep for up to 1 month, stored in an airtight container in the freezer. Or half-fill a martini glass or small tumbler with some of the granita, add a couple ounces of gin or vodka, and sip it alongside the oysters. | **Makes 6 to 8 servings**

Grapefruit-Campari Granita

- 1½ cups strained freshly squeezed grapefruit juice
- ⅓ cup Campari
- 1 tablespoon sugar
- ¼ teaspoon finely grated grapefruit zest
- Pinch of kosher salt or flaky or coarse sea salt

- 2 dozen small to medium oysters, shell scrubbed
- Rock salt, for serving

To make the granita, stir together the juice, Campari, sugar, zest, and salt in a small bowl until the sugar is dissolved. Pour into a shallow dish, such as a pie plate, and freeze until it begins to set around the edges, 35 to 45 minutes. Remove from the freezer and draw the tines of a fork through the mixture a number of times to break up the forming ice crystals, crushing larger pieces under the fork. Continue freezing the mixture, stirring every 15 to 20 minutes, until it is fully frozen and has a light, flaky texture, about 2 hours total.

Just before serving, use an oyster knife to shuck the oysters. I like to fold a thick dish towel in quarters and nestle the oyster (cupped side down) between folds of the towel, with the back hinged end exposed. Use the tip of the oyster knife to wedge carefully between the oyster halves at or near the hinge, then slide the blade in, flat against the inside of the top shell. As you slide the oyster knife blade across the shell, you'll cut through one of the adductor muscles that's holding the shell halves together. Lift off and discard the top shell and gently slide the knife blade under the oyster as well, to slice through the lower adductor muscle. Please be very careful to avoid slipping as both the oyster shell and knife can do harm.

Top a platter with an inch or so of rock salt. Set the half shell oysters on the platter, nestling the shells evenly down into the salt. Take the granita from the freezer, scrape it again with a fork to loosen it, and top each oyster with a generous teaspoonful. Serve right away.

Smoked Salmon Rillettes

This recipe is a fish-lover's interpretation of the classic French bistro and café fare *rillettes de porc*. Should you have some leftover grilled salmon on hand, it can replace up to half of the smoked salmon. I prefer to use hot-smoked salmon here rather than cold-smoked salmon. Sometimes called "kippered" salmon, it is prepared with gentle but direct smoky heat, leaving it with a firm, moist, flaky texture that's ideal for this recipe.

If you're in the market for a homemade cracker to serve with these rillettes, you have more than a few choices in this book! I recommend The Best Crackers (page 64), Rye Crackers with Caraway (page 76), or Modern Melba (page 80). For embellishment, you can top the rillettes with a scattering of capers just before serving. | **Makes 6 to 8 servings**

1/2 cup unsalted butter, at room temperature

1/4 cup cream cheese, at room temperature

8 ounces hot-smoked salmon, skin removed

2 tablespoons dry vermouth or dry white wine, more if needed

Pinch of freshly grated or ground nutmeg

Kosher salt or flaky or coarse sea salt

Freshly ground white or black pepper

Crackers, baguette slices, and/or cucumber slices, for serving

Cream together the butter and cream cheese in a large bowl with a wooden spoon until well blended and smooth. Finely flake the smoked salmon into the bowl, discarding any bones you come across. Add the vermouth and nutmeg, stirring well. Taste for seasoning, adding salt and pepper to taste. The texture should be smooth and spreadable. If the mixture is quite stiff, stir in a bit more vermouth.

Spoon the rillettes into a single serving bowl or individual ramekins, cover well with plastic wrap, and refrigerate for at least 2 hours before serving, to allow the flavors to meld. The rillettes can be made up to 3 days in advance.

About 30 minutes before serving, take the rillettes from the refrigerator and set on the counter to soften a bit. Serve with small knives for spreading onto the crackers, baguette slices, and/or cucumber slices.

Smoked Salmon *with Ginger and Black Pepper*

Choose a salmon fillet piece that has an even thickness, preferably from near the head end of the fish rather than the thinner tail end. Salmon is most commonly smoked in large pieces, but here the fish is first cut into slender strips to smoke, leaving you with perfect finger-friendly smoked salmon to snack on. I most often used alderwood chips for smoking salmon, though apple wood is another good option. For the grated ginger here, I find the small holes on a standard box grater work well. I like to grate it directly into the saucepan before the other brine ingredients are added, so all the juices that run from the ginger are captured as well.

If you ever find yourself with an abundance of salmon on hand—a fisherman in the family perhaps?—then you might try an even more luscious approach. The lower belly portion of each fillet generally has richer striations of fat, which makes for particularly delicious smoked salmon. If you have the luxury of this option, cut lengthwise strips from that belly meat, saving the top portion for another use. | **Makes 6 to 8 servings**

---

3 cups water

1 cup packed light brown sugar

²/₃ cup kosher salt or flaky or coarse sea salt

¹/₃ cup finely grated fresh ginger

1 tablespoon coarsely ground black pepper, plus more for sprinkling

1 salmon fillet piece (about 1¹/₂ pounds), skin and pin bones removed

Combine the water, brown sugar, salt, ginger, and pepper in a medium saucepan and bring just to a boil over medium-high heat, stirring occasionally to help the sugar and salt dissolve. Take the pan from the heat and let cool to room temperature. While the brine is cooling, cut the salmon fillet crosswise into slices about ¹/₂ inch thick.

Pour the cooled brine into a large shallow dish, such as a 9 by 13-inch baking dish. Add the salmon strips, pressing down gently so they're well coated with the brine. Cover the dish with plastic wrap and refrigerate for about 3 hours. Take the fish from the brine, rinse lightly under cold water, and dry well with paper towels. Set the salmon pieces on a wire rack, sprinkle the tops lightly with pepper, and let air dry on the counter until the surface is no longer sticky, about 1 hour. If you have a small fan, set it up to blow gently on the salmon to speed up the drying a bit.

About 30 minutes before you are ready to smoke, put 2 cups of wood chips in a bowl and cover with cold water. Set aside to soak.

Preheat a batch of charcoal in your grill (if you have a gas grill or smoker, prepare it for smoking according to manufacturer's instructions). When the coals are glowing, pour them into two small mounds on opposite sides of the grill. Put a small disposable aluminum pan on the rack between the two piles of coals and add a couple inches of water to the pan. Quickly but thoroughly drain the wood chips and scatter them over the charcoal. Set the grill grate on the grill and lightly brush the grate with oil. Lay the salmon pieces as much toward the center of the grate as you can, not over the coals, and cover with the lid. Smoke until the salmon is cooked through and the fish has an amber hue from the smoke, about 15 minutes.

Take the salmon from the grill and let cool. Arrange the salmon strips on a platter for serving, or store in an airtight container and refrigerate for up to 3 days before serving.

SMOKING

Most any outdoor covered grill can be used for smoking. It's important to set up indirect heat so that the fish cooks a bit more gently than with traditional grilling. My classic kettle-style Weber doubles as a good smoker. I offer instructions here for a standard grill, but if you have a smoker by all means use it. Smoking time will vary with the thickness of the fish you use, the type of smoker, level of heat, outdoor temperature, and other variables, so keep your eye on things and judge more by the fish than by the timer. Smoking is as much art as science.

Pickled Trout *with Horseradish Sauce*

When I was a kid, one thing in our refrigerator I was never tempted to sneak a taste of was the jar of pickled herring that was always on one of the door's shelves, ready for my dad to dip into on a whim. But the memory of that herring is one I relish, one that had me thinking of my dad often on our trip a few years ago to Stockholm, where the art of pickling herring and other fish is raised to a true art form. This recipe, using easier-to-find and more mildly flavored trout, is a tribute that favorite snack I grew up watching Dad enjoy so much.

In place of the thinly sliced rye bread, you could make a batch of the Rye Crackers with Caraway on page 76 for serving. If you're unable to find fresh horseradish, you can simply omit it from the pickling mixture and use jarred horseradish for the sauce. This same pickling principle works well with a salmon fillet, preferably thinner fillet portions cut across in $3/4$-inch strips as for the trout. Larger fillets can be cut into $3/4$-inch cubes. | **Makes 6 to 8 servings**

1½ cups white distilled vinegar

½ cup water

¼ cup kosher salt or flaky or coarse sea salt

1 tablespoon sugar

1 (2-inch) piece fresh horseradish, peeled and thinly sliced

1 shallot, thinly sliced

3 large cloves garlic, thinly sliced

2 tablespoons juniper berries

1 tablespoon coriander seeds

2 teaspoons whole black peppercorns

3 bay leaves, preferably fresh

12 ounces trout fillets, skin and pin bones removed (see next page)

Horseradish Sauce

¼ cup sour cream

2 tablespoons finely grated fresh horseradish or prepared horseradish

Pinch of kosher salt or flaky or coarse sea salt

Combine the vinegar, water, salt, and sugar in a medium saucepan and bring just to a boil over medium-high heat, stirring occasionally to help the sugar and salt dissolve. Add the sliced horseradish, shallot, garlic, juniper berries, coriander seeds, peppercorns, and bay leaves and simmer over medium-low heat for 5 minutes. Set aside to cool to nearly room temperature.

While the pickling liquid is cooling, cut each trout fillet across into $3/4$-inch pieces. Put the trout in a medium nonreactive bowl, preferably one that's somewhat tall, rather than broad and flat, for best results. Pour the barely warm pickling liquid over and gently stir the mixture to be sure everything's well blended. Cover the bowl with plastic wrap and refrigerate for at least 24 hours and up to 48 hours.

---

continued on next page

To make the sauce, stir together the sour cream, horseradish, and salt in a small bowl. Cover and refrigerate until you are ready to serve. It can be made a day or two ahead, though it will become stronger in flavor as time passes.

Before serving, use a slotted spoon to lift the trout from the pickling liquid into a serving bowl. The shallot and garlic can be served with the trout, but discard the other seasonings. Serve with the sauce alongside.

REMOVING PIN BONES AND SKIN FROM FISH FILLETS

The tool I turn to for removing pin bones from a fish such as trout or salmon was long ago snagged from the tool chest and recommissioned for this sole purpose: a small pair of needle-nose pliers. They're the best way I've found to secure a good grip on those small bones and have leverage to tug them out effectively. The bones are set in the flesh at a slight angle and can be hard to see. Run your fingers down the length of the fish fillet, from tail end toward the head, and you should feel the tips of the bones (note that they don't run all the way to the tail). Grab the tip of a bone with the pliers and gently tug. Sometimes despite my best efforts, the tip of the bone may break off, in which case I just feel around for the tip of the remaining portion of bone and nab the rest of it. If all else fails, simply warn your guests that there may be a rogue bone or two in the finished dish. It just takes a few minutes, and is not an obligatory step, but it is one that helps keep guests from having to work their way around fish bones when eating.

To remove the skin from the fillet, set it skin-side down on the cutting board with the tail end toward you and the other end of the fish pointing away at about a 45 degree angle toward your right side if you're right-handed, otherwise toward your left. With the hand that's not holding your knife (choose a thin-bladed sharp knife), hold the tip of the tail end of the fish securely against the cutting board and make a shallow, downward cut into the flesh just in front of your fingers. Just before the blade reaches the skin of the fish, turn the blade to a nearly horizontal level. With gentle strokes in a back-and-forth sawing motion, move the knife blade between the skin and the flesh toward the broader end of the fillet. Continue to hold the skin down securely with the other hand, so the knife slides through easily while the flesh and the skin stay more or less in place.

Salt Cod *and* Potato Puffs

These puffs are a finger food twist on *brandade*, which is often served warm in a ramekin to spread onto crackers or bread. Look for salt cod at specialty seafood markets or in the seafood department of well-stocked grocery stores, sometimes in the freezer section. And be sure to plan ahead as the cod needs to soak overnight before being used. | **Makes about 32 puffs**

---

8 ounces salt cod

2 russet potatoes (about 1½ pounds), scrubbed and quartered

2 large eggs, lightly beaten

½ cup finely chopped green onions, white and pale green portions

1 tablespoon finely minced or pressed garlic

Kosher salt or flaky or coarse sea salt and freshly ground white pepper

Vegetable oil, for frying

Rinse off the surface salt from the salt cod under cold running water. Put the salt cod in a medium bowl and add cold water to cover by a couple of inches. Cover the bowl and refrigerate for 24 hours, changing the water four or five times. Drain well.

Put the fish in a saucepan of fresh cold water. Bring to a boil over medium-high heat, then reduce to medium and simmer until tender, about 15 minutes. Drain and let cool. Finely flake the fish with your fingers; set aside on paper towels to continue draining while you cook the potatoes.

Put the potatoes in a pan of cold salted water and bring just to a boil over medium-high heat. Reduce the heat to medium and simmer gently until the potatoes are tender when pierced with the tip of a knife, 15 to 20 minutes; the water shouldn't boil vigorously, so reduce the heat to medium-low, if needed. Drain the potatoes and let cool, then peel away the skin and cut the potatoes into chunks.

Use a ricer or potato masher to thoroughly mash the potatoes in a bowl. Add the fish to the potatoes with the eggs, green onions, and garlic. Season lightly with salt and pepper and stir well to evenly mix the ingredients. (Even though you're using "salt" cod, much of the salt has been drawn off by the soaking and the simmering; I found the puffs bland without a bit of additional salt.)

Pour about 2 inches of oil into a large heavy saucepan (the oil should not come more than halfway up the sides of the pan). Bring to 365°F over medium heat. Using a 1½-inch spring-type ice cream scoop or 2 small spoons, form the potato mixture into bite-size balls and gently add them—6 or 7 at a time—to the hot oil. Cook, turning once or twice, until evenly and lightly browned, 4 to 5 minutes. Use a slotted spoon to transfer the puffs to paper towels to drain while cooking the remaining mixture in batches, allowing the oil to reheat between batches as needed.

Arrange the puffs on a plate and serve. For a clean-fingers option, spear each puff on a toothpick.

Sesame Chicken Bites

I don't know why this screams "midnight snack" to me, but it does. If you plan ahead for those late-night munchies—maybe for when you land back at home after an evening out carousing with your pals—you'll have marinated the chicken in the afternoon and have nothing more to do than quickly toss the pieces in sesame seeds, pop them on a baking sheet, and slip them into the oven for 10 minutes or so. Sure beats another bowl of cold cereal before bed.

| **Makes 6 to 8 servings**

2 large boneless, skinless chicken breasts (about 1 1/2 pounds)

3 tablespoons soy sauce

1 tablespoon toasted sesame oil

1 teaspoon finely grated fresh ginger

Pinch of red pepper flakes

1/2 cup white sesame seeds

Cut the chicken breasts into 1 1/4-inch cubes and put them in a medium bowl. Add the soy sauce, sesame oil, ginger, and pepper flakes and stir well to evenly coat the chicken. Cover and refrigerate for 1 to 4 hours.

Preheat the oven to 425°F. Line a rimmed baking sheet with foil or parchment paper.

Put the sesame seeds in a shallow dish. Lift a couple pieces of the chicken at a time from the marinade, allowing excess to drip off. Quickly coat the chicken in sesame seeds, patting to remove excess, and set them on the baking sheet. Repeat with the remaining chicken pieces. Bake until lightly browned and no longer pink in the center, 8 to 10 minutes.

Pierce each piece of chicken with the tip of a frilly toothpick or mini skewer and arrange the chicken bites on a plate or platter for serving.

Five-Spice Duck Skin

These duck skins cook down to almost nothing, since much of their weight is in the form of fat that seeps off while cooking (see box). But the little curls of crisped skin that are left pack a lot of rich flavor in a tiny bite—like pork cracklins but with a distinctive Asian touch. It's a great use for the skins you've removed before making the Duck Jerky on page 102, or any time you'd like to get double-duty from duck breasts. | **Makes 2 to 4 servings**

1¹/₂ teaspoons toasted sesame oil

Skin from 4 to 6 small or 2 large duck breasts (8 to 10 ounces total)

1 tablespoon five-spice powder

1 teaspoon kosher salt or flaky or coarse sea salt

Rub the sesame oil evenly over both sides of the duck skin. Sprinkle the five-spice powder and salt over both sides of the duck skin and use your fingers to rub the spices evenly over the skin. Arrange the skin on a plate in a single layer and refrigerate, uncovered, for 2 hours to allow the seasonings to be absorbed and the skin to dry out a bit.

Cut the skin crosswise into ¹/₂-inch strips. Heat a cast-iron skillet or other large heavy skillet over medium heat. Add the duck skin strips and cook, stirring occasionally, until there's about ¹/₄ inch of rendered fat in the bottom of the skillet, 1 to 2 minutes. Reduce the heat to medium-low and continue cooking until the skin is evenly browned and crisp, 12 to 15 minutes, stirring occasionally. Scoop out the crisped skin to paper towels to drain, then transfer to a small bowl. The crisped skin will be best enjoyed the day it is prepared.

DUCK FAT—YUM

You may be a little shocked at how much liquid fat renders from the duck skin while it cooks. But consider yourself blessed; many chefs consider this to be liquid, delicious gold. Strain the fat through a coffee filter or cheesecloth-lined fine sieve; discard the lingering spices. Store the fat in the refrigerator in an airtight container for a month or two.

I've got a couple of specific suggestions in this book for using the fat: Duck Fat Potato Chips on page 20, or as an alternative to the melted butter in the Herbes de Provence Crackers on page 71. Classically, it's magical as the means for sautéing potatoes, or most any vegetable.

Duck Jerky

No longer the afterthought snack of tooth-jarring dried meat at the convenience store check-out, jerky has been gaining appreciation as a snack of delightful diversity. Of all the meaty options, duck is one that I find has a wonderful rich and savory flavor, with a pleasantly tender texture. You can use either larger moulard duck breasts or smaller Pekin or Long Island duck breasts for this recipe, which means you may be starting with as few as 2 breasts or as many as 6 from the smaller ducks. Note that the skin can—or should, really—be used for the Five-Spice Duck Skin (page 101). And I list a couple of options there, too, for using the duck fat that you'll be left with from that recipe. So despite the fact that whole duck breasts can be a bit spendy, once you've got them in hand you'll have a few different delicious snacks to make from them.

If you have a dehydrator, this is a great time to use it, following manufacturer's instructions.

| **Makes 6 to 8 servings**

---

2 pounds boneless duck breasts

1/2 cup minced onion

2 tablespoons chipotle en adobo

2 tablespoons honey

2 teaspoons kosher salt or flaky or coarse sea salt

1 teaspoon freshly ground black pepper

1/2 cup chicken broth

1/4 cup Worcestershire sauce

3 long strips orange zest

Use the tip of a small sharp knife to help separate the skin from the meat of the duck breasts, starting at one end of the breast and sliding the knife tip along the line where skin meets breast, gently pulling away the skin as you go. Discard or save the skin for another use. Put the duck breasts on a plate and freeze until firm but not fully frozen, about 30 minutes.

While the duck is freezing, combine the onion, chipotle, honey, salt, and pepper in a blender or mini food processor and pulse until well blended and nearly smooth. Transfer this to a large resealable plastic bag (see box) or large bowl. Add the chicken broth to the blender or processor bowl and swirl it around a bit to help release any remaining puree, then add this to the bag along with the Worcestershire sauce and orange zest.

Use a sharp knife to cut the duck breasts lengthwise into $3/8$-inch slices. Add them to the marinade 1 or 2 at a time to help assure that they do not stick together, so the marinade evenly coats all the pieces. Carefully seal the bag, or cover the bowl with plastic wrap, and refrigerate overnight, or up to 24 hours. Turn the bag over or stir the meat a few times, to ensure the duck slices marinate evenly.

The next day, preheat the oven to 170°F. Line 2 rimmed baking sheets with foil or silicone baking mats (parchment paper doesn't work well in this case).

Lift the duck slices from the marinade and lay them on paper towels, patting the tops with more paper towels to dry the meat. Arrange the duck slices on the baking sheets; they'll shrink as they dry, so the pieces can be snug, but avoid letting them overlap.

Dry the duck in the oven until the slices have darkened and feel leathery, 4 to 5 hours. After the first hour, turn the duck slices over and return the baking sheets to the same racks. After the second hour, switch the baking sheets to opposite racks. After the third hour, once again turn the slices to ensure even drying.

Set the duck jerky aside to cool on the baking sheets, then transfer to a bowl for serving, or store in an airtight container in the refrigerator for up to 1 week.

A LITTLE SUPPORT

Without an extra pair of hands in the kitchen to help out, it can be a challenge to work with those big resealable plastic bags when you're maneuvering ingredients. Here's my trick to make the process easier. First, I fold down the top edge of the bag, which helps naturally broaden the top of the bag for easier access. Then I grab a large mixing bowl and put the bag upright in the bowl, pressing the bottom of the bag down with the palm of my hand to help create a somewhat flat base. The sides of the bowl help support the bag and, should things still slip, at least the bag contents will collect in the bowl, rather than all over your counter. Now you've got two hands free to add other ingredients to the bag or whatever else you need to do before sealing up the bag.

Salami Chips *with Grainy Mustard Dip*

This recipe is so easy, I'm almost embarrassed to include it in a cookbook. But it just goes to prove how much transformation can come from the simple act of crisping something in the oven for a bit (see kale chips on page 24). Try to find a salami that's $1^1/_2$ to $2^1/_2$ inches in diameter, for easy snacking size. If it's not presliced and there's a deli slicer in the store, ask to have it thinly sliced for you. Otherwise do your best to cut very thin, even slices with your sharpest knife.

    I like the combination of traditional Dijon mustard and grainy mustard for the dip, but if you prefer you can use just one type or the other. The flavor of the dip will be best if it's made at least 2 hours ahead, allowing the flavors to meld nicely before serving. | **Makes 6 to 8 servings**

Grainy Mustard Dip

- $^1/_4$ cup sour cream
- $^1/_4$ cup top-quality mayonnaise
- 2 tablespoons Dijon mustard
- 2 tablespoons grainy mustard

- 8 ounces thinly sliced salami

To make the dip, stir together the sour cream, mayonnaise, Dijon mustard, and grainy mustard in a small serving bowl. Cover with plastic wrap and refrigerate until you are ready to serve, ideally at least 2 hours.

    Preheat the oven to 375°F. Line 2 rimmed baking sheets with parchment paper or silicone baking mats. Set 2 oven racks at the center-most positions.

    Lay the salami slices out in a single layer on the baking sheets. Bake until they are evenly browned and rigid, 10 to 12 minutes. Transfer to paper towels to drain and cool. The salami will crisp further as it cools.

    Arrange the salami chips in a bowl or on a plate, with the dip alongside.

SALAMI

Feel free to play around with different types of salami for this recipe. I'm lucky to live in the hometown of Salumi, the little sliver of meat-lover's heaven here in Seattle, founded by master salumist Armandino Batali and carried on today by his daughter Gina Batali and son-in-law Brian D'Amato. I love the results from crisping up the *sopressata* and *finocchiona* from Salumi for this snack. I've noticed Salumi products in some top-flight delis and specialty food shops around the country. But use any really good salami you can find. I've also used mainstream salami available at the grocery store with decent results as well.

Deviled Bacon

Bacon's already devilishly good on its own; you don't need me to tell you that crisp bacon is an ideal snack. But when you want to take it to another level, here's one sure bet. And it is a quick one to boot, with nice zing from the mustard and hot sauce that complement bacon's richness. | **Makes 6 to 8 servings**

---

3 tablespoons Worcestershire sauce

2 tablespoons Dijon mustard

2 teaspoons Tabasco sauce, or 1 teaspoon sriracha

3/4 pound thick-cut bacon, each slice halved crosswise

Stir together the Worcestershire sauce, mustard, and Tabasco in a small bowl until smooth.

Preheat the oven to 400°F. Line a rimmed baking sheet with foil.

If the bacon you're using is a bit watery, sandwich it between 2 double-layers of paper towels and press well on the top to help remove excess water; this will help assure crispest results later.

Arrange the bacon strips on the baking sheet, avoiding overlap. Spoon about half of the mustard mixture over the bacon pieces, spreading it out with the back of the spoon. Bake the bacon until lightly browned on top, 12 to 15 minutes. Take the pan from the oven, turn the bacon pieces over, and spoon the remaining mustard mixture over the bacon slices. Return the pan to the oven and bake until the bacon is nicely glazed, moderately browned, and crisp, about 15 minutes longer. If some pieces around the outer edge of the pan are browning more quickly, remove them earlier.

Transfer the bacon pieces to a piece of paper towel to drain for a few minutes, then transfer to a plate or platter for serving. Serve warm or at room temperature. The deviled bacon will be best served shortly after baking.

Crisp Beef *with Lemongrass*

This recipe is inspired by a preparation from Southeast Asia, where traditionally the beef might be dried in the sun. Unlike jerky, which cooks meat low and slow to dry it out gradually, this hot-oven version cooks the thinly sliced beef more quickly, with crisper results.

Try to find presliced thin beef, as for sukiyaki, shabu-shabu, or other hot-pot preparations. In Seattle I can buy thinly sliced meat from different cuts of beef—ribeye, chuck eye steak, eye of round—at Asian markets, such as Uwajimaya. As you'll have no trim or waste, 3/4 pound of this sliced meat will be plenty. Otherwise buy sirloin or flatiron steak, preferably at least 1 1/2 inches thick; plan to start with 1 pound as you're likely to have some trim and the slices will surely be a bit thicker. Freeze the meat until it is firm but not fully frozen, 30 to 45 minutes, then cut across the grain into thin slices, as close to 1/16 inch as you can get. But the thin, even slices of the store-sliced beef are unbeatable for ease and the crispest results. | **Makes 4 to 6 servings**

---

3 tablespoons finely chopped lemongrass
3 tablespoons chopped green onion tops
2 teaspoons finely minced or pressed garlic
1/4 cup water
3 tablespoons Asian fish sauce
3/4 to 1 pound very thinly sliced beef

Combine the lemongrass, green onion, and garlic in a food processor (a mini if you have one, see page 10) and puree until very finely chopped and well blended. Add the water and fish sauce and blend well. Transfer the marinade to a medium bowl or large resealable plastic bag (see box, page 103). Add the beef slices to the marinade, 1 or 2 at a time to help assure that they do not stick together, so the marinade evenly coats all the pieces. Cover the bowl with plastic wrap or carefully seal the bag and marinate in the refrigerator for 4 to 5 hours.

When you are ready to cook the meat, preheat the oven to 450°F. Line 2 rimmed baking sheets with foil or silicone baking mats. Set 2 oven racks at the centermost positions.

Lift the beef slices from the marinade, allowing any excess liquid to drip off. Arrange some (likely about half) of the slices in an even layer on the prepared baking sheets; the meat will shrink quite a lot as it cooks, so the pieces can be snug but avoid overlapping. Bake until the meat is moderately brown (more mahogany than deep brown) and rigid, about 15 minutes, turning the meat slices and switching the pans on the racks about halfway through. Transfer the beef to a cooling rack; it will crisp further as it cools. Repeat with the remaining beef, replacing the foil or cleaning the baking mats first if needed. The high oven temperature tends to singe the juices that run off from the meat.

Transfer the beef crisps to a bowl. They will be best enjoyed the day they are made.

Nuts and Nibbles

This is some dangerous territory in the following pages. Many of these recipes are of the type that if you make a batch and no one's around to share it with, you might find yourself going back for "just one more handful" so many times the bowl's soon empty. Nuts and popcorn are frequent culprits, both of which get some tasty interpretations here. I even play around with little quail eggs and tofu to help show just how diverse the realm of salty snacks can be.

Toasted Walnuts *with* Tart Cherries and Rosemary

My friend Kay Simon, winemaker and co-owner with husband Clay Mackey of Chinook Wines in eastern Washington, coaxed me into creating this recipe. She was telling me one day about the productive walnut trees they'd been harvesting on their property and as an aside lamented that so many commercial nut mixes and toasted nut recipes include a good dose of sugar. Witness the ubiquitous "candied walnut" that graces countless salads and cheese trays.

Like her, I'm perplexed that toasted nuts so often are sweet. For her winery tasting room in Prosser, Washington, she likes to serve the nuts in preparations that let the savory character of the nut shine through—which nudged me to come up with this combination, using all-natural tart dried cherries from fellow Prosser-based company Chukar Cherries (page 153). This pairs particularly well with Chinook's beloved Cabernet Franc rosé wine but is a generally wine-friendly snack to go with whatever you're pouring! | **Makes about 3 cups**

2¹/₂ cups walnut halves

2 tablespoons unsalted butter, melted

2 tablespoons finely minced fresh rosemary

1 teaspoon kosher salt or flaky or coarse sea salt

¹/₂ teaspoon freshly ground black pepper

³/₄ cup dried tart cherries

Preheat the oven to 350°F.

Put the walnuts in a medium bowl and drizzle the butter over, tossing well to evenly coat the nuts. Add the rosemary, salt, and pepper and toss well to evenly mix. Spread the nuts out on a rimmed baking sheet. Bake until the nuts smell toasty and are just lightly browned, 12 to 14 minutes, stirring a few times to ensure even cooking.

Transfer the nuts to a bowl (it can be the same one they were first mixed in), add the dried cherries, and toss to mix. Let cool, then transfer to a serving bowl or store in an airtight container for up to 5 days.

Popcorn *with Chili-Lime Butter and Cotija*

From the simple starting point of a bowl of popcorn, snackers have a potentially endless array of ways to exercise flavor-induced creativity. Any number of spices—smoked paprika, curry powder, cumin—can simply be sprinkled over, with a bit of melted butter or good olive oil to help them adhere when tossed. Minced fresh herbs, finely grated cheese, flakes of nori (dried seaweed). Hmmmm, you might even try the Peanut Dukka on page 83! This recipe with lime zest, chili powder, and salty cotija cheese is just one many possible tasty combos. | **Makes 10 cups**

- 10 cups popped popcorn (about 5 tablespoons kernels)
- ¼ cup unsalted butter
- 1 tablespoon chili powder
- 1 teaspoon finely grated lime zest
- ½ cup finely grated cotija cheese
- ½ teaspoon kosher salt or flaky or coarse sea salt

Put the popcorn in a large bowl. Melt the butter in a small saucepan and stir in the chili powder and lime zest. Set aside for 5 to 10 minutes to allow the flavors to meld a bit. Stir the melted butter mixture to blend and drizzle it over the popcorn, tossing well to evenly coat. Add the cotija cheese and salt and again toss to evenly mix with the popcorn. Serve right away.

POPCORN HISTORY

Popcorn is among the earliest snack foods we enjoyed in the United States. And there's little wonder why popcorn has so fully caught our snacking fancy. Once dried, the popcorn kernels keep well. And popcorn is so easy to make; long ago it was as simple as tossing a whole dried ear of popcorn onto a fire and doing your best to catch or gather the popped kernels that flew out of the embers. Eventually, long-handled wire baskets were developed that allowed loose kernels to pop within a confined space for much more efficient (if far less sporting) results.

With the advent of steam-powered popping machines that street vendors began using on colorful carts in the late 1800s, the snack began to follow us to fairs, ballparks, and other gathering places. We've long associated popcorn with the movie-going experience, but many early movie houses weren't too keen on the potential mess and distraction of indoor eating. So for a number of years, patrons would find a popcorn cart stationed outside the theater to meet their snacking needs. Over time, however, theater owners realized they were missing the boat on (what has grown to become serious) revenue potential. So they began setting up their own popcorn machines and selling it themselves, along with roasted peanuts and other treats. The rest is snacking history. It's nearly impossible to avoid the lure of that tub of fluffy popcorn as we head for our seats to catch the latest movie release.

TV Snack Mix

"TV mixes" or "TV snack mixes" were recipes developed in the mid-twentieth century as convenient and tasty snacks to enjoy for uninterrupted TV watching, long before the "pause" or "record" button had been invented. You've probably heard of one of them? The ubiquitous Chex Mix recipe was launched in the early 1950s and is still printed on cereal boxes today. Timeless and still beloved. When feeling super lazy, I'll even pick up the bag of premade Chex Mix at the store. This is my variation on the theme. The oyster crackers I use are the small dime-size puffed crackers commonly scattered over seafood chowders or stews. | **Makes about 4 cups**

1^1/$_2$ cups Kix cereal

1 cup Wheat Chex cereal

1 cup oyster crackers

^{1}/$_2$ cup roasted whole peanuts or coarsely chopped hazelnuts

^{1}/$_3$ cup unsalted butter

3 tablespoons Worcestershire sauce

1 teaspoon ground coriander

1 teaspoon powdered mustard

1 teaspoon sweet Hungarian paprika

1 teaspoon kosher salt or flaky or coarse sea salt

Preheat the oven to 300°F.

Combine the Kix, Wheat Chex, oyster crackers, and peanuts in a large bowl.

Melt the butter in a small saucepan, then stir in the Worcestershire sauce, ground coriander, powdered mustard, paprika, and salt. Drizzle the seasoned butter over the cereal mixture and toss well to evenly mix. Scatter the mixture in a rimmed baking sheet.

Bake until aromatic and toasty, 30 to 40 minutes, stirring occasionally. Set aside to cool, then transfer to a serving bowl, or store in an airtight container for up to 3 days.

Orange-Roasted Pecans

There's a touch of sweet and savory going on in this recipe, with the combination of orange juice and black pepper. They both complement slightly rich, slightly sweet pecans in an ideal fashion. | **Makes about 3 cups**

---

  1 tablespoon finely grated orange zest
  1 cup freshly squeezed orange juice
  1 tablespoon light brown sugar
  3 cups pecan halves
  1 1/2 teaspoons kosher salt or flaky or coarse sea salt
  1/2 teaspoon freshly ground black pepper

Preheat the oven to 350°F. Line a rimmed baking sheet with parchment paper or a silicone baking mat.

Combine the orange zest, orange juice, and brown sugar in a medium saucepan and bring just to a boil over medium-high heat, stirring occasionally to help the sugar dissolve. Reduce the heat to medium and boil until reduced by about half, 5 to 7 minutes.

Add the pecans, salt, and pepper to the pan and stir the nuts gently into the orange mixture. Continue to cook over medium heat, stirring often, until the liquid is reduced to a glaze and evenly coats the nuts, 6 to 8 minutes.

Transfer the nuts to the baking sheet, spreading them out in a single layer. Bake until aromatic and nicely browned, 20 to 25 minutes, stirring every 5 minutes or so to ensure even toasting. Keep a close eye on the nuts near the end; they may need to be stirred more often and can go from "nicely browned" to "a bit burned" pretty quickly. Set aside to cool completely, stirring occasionally to avoid sticking.

Transfer the pecans to a serving bowl or, if not serving within a few hours, store them in an airtight container for up to 1 week.

Salted Popcorn Meringues

Sure, meringues are generally in the "sweets" category, and for good reason. Without a minimum of sugar added to the whipped egg whites, the traditional chemistry just doesn't work in favor of the airy foam remaining light and delicate when baked. So this is one of those yin-yang treats pairing sweet with salty-popcorn flavor. Oh, and it's a surprisingly tasty one at that.

| **Makes about 4 dozen meringues**

2/3 cup sugar

1 tablespoon cornstarch

1 teaspoon kosher salt or flaky or coarse sea salt

3 large egg whites

1 1/2 tablespoons white vinegar

1 1/2 cups finely ground popped popcorn (see box)

Preheat the oven to 225°F. Line 2 baking sheets with parchment paper or silicone baking mats. Set 2 oven racks at the centermost positions.

Stir together the sugar, cornstarch, and 1/2 teaspoon of the salt in a small dish. Combine the egg whites and vinegar in the bowl of a stand mixer fitted with the whip attachment. Blend at medium speed until quite frothy, 1 to 2 minutes. Increase the speed to medium-high and begin gradually adding the sugar mixture. Continue beating until all the sugar has been added and the egg whites are glossy and firm, about 2 minutes longer. Take the bowl from the mixer, sprinkle the ground popcorn over, and gently but thoroughly fold it into the meringue.

Spoon the meringue mixture into a pastry bag fitted with a large plain tip. Pipe the mixture in about 1 1/2-inch mounds on the baking sheets. Sprinkle a bit of the remaining salt over each meringue. Bake until firm but still pale in color, 1 1/2 to 2 hours, switching the pans about halfway through for even cooking. Take the pans from the oven and let cool completely before removing the meringues.

Store them in an airtight container until you are ready to serve. The meringues will be best served the same day they are made.

THE POPCORN GRIND

To get that surprising flavor of popcorn in such an unexpected package as a meringue, it's as easy as making popcorn and taking it for a spin in the food processor. For the best flavor, the popcorn should be unseasoned. I still make popcorn on the stove top in a pan—I'm kind of old school that way. If you're using microwave popcorn, I recommend choosing a plain type, with minimal to no butter "flavor" or excess salt. Oils and other additives in the popcorn can, when folded into the egg whites, deflate their glossy firm texture a bit. I tested this recipe once with Newman's Own Butter Microwave Popcorn and the results were tasty, but the meringues were a bit flatter.

It's worth the extra few minutes to pick out any unpopped or just partially popped kernels before processing the popcorn. Not only would they be unpleasant to bite into in one of the meringues, any large or hard pieces may block the piping bag when forming the meringues.

Put about $2^1/2$ cups of the fluffy, well-popped popcorn in a food processor and pulse until very finely ground, which may take 1 to 2 minutes.

Caramel-Masala Popcorn *and* Pistachios

Garam masala is an Indian spice blend that can include a range of spices such as black pepper, cloves, cumin, nutmeg, and cardamom. It makes for an intriguing counterpoint to the inherent sweetness of caramel corn, which was one of my early culinary specialties. As a teenager, I made countless batches of traditional caramel corn to not only share with my family but also to bag up and share with friends at the holidays. It was fun to revisit that favorite recipe with a new salty-savory twist. | **Makes 6 to 8 servings**

---

8 cups popped popcorn (about $1/4$ cup kernels)

1 cup chopped toasted pistachios

$1/2$ cup unsalted butter

2 tablespoons garam masala

1 cup packed light brown sugar

$1/4$ cup light corn syrup

1 teaspoon baking soda

1 teaspoon fleur de sel, coarse or flaky sea salt, or kosher salt

Preheat the oven to 250°F. Put the popcorn in a large baking dish, roasting pan, or broiler pan and scatter the pistachios over; set aside.

Melt the butter in a medium saucepan over medium heat. Add the garam masala and cook, stirring, until quite aromatic, about 1 minute. Add the brown sugar and corn syrup and cook, stirring often, until the sugar has dissolved and the mixture comes just to a boil. Once it reaches a boil, continue cooking for 3 to 4 minutes, stirring constantly. Take the pan from the heat and stir in the baking soda, which will lighten and expand the mixture. Pour the caramel mixture over the popcorn and

pistachios and stir to combine. Sprinkle the salt evenly over the popcorn. (Don't worry about the caramel not evenly coating the popcorn at this point.)

Bake the popcorn for 1 hour, taking the pan from the oven every 15 minutes to stir the popcorn well and help distribute the caramel evenly. Set the pan aside to cool, stirring occasionally to avoid sticking. When cool, transfer the caramel corn to a serving bowl.

If you are not serving the popcorn within a few hours, store it in an airtight container for 1 to 2 days.

Mixed Nuts Mole

A touch of cocoa powder, some spice from chile powder, sesame seeds, and a hint of garlic—the flavors of traditional Oaxacan mole sauce play out quite nicely as a seasoning for roasted mixed nuts. | **Makes about 3 cups**

1 tablespoon unsweetened cocoa powder

1 teaspoon kosher salt or flaky or coarse sea salt

1 teaspoon sugar

3/4 teaspoon cayenne or other hot chile powder

3/4 teaspoon garlic powder or garlic granules (not garlic salt)

3 cups unsalted nuts (peanuts, pecan halves, walnut halves, whole or slivered almonds, and/or hazelnuts)

1/2 cup unsalted hulled (green) pumpkin seeds

2 tablespoon white sesame seeds

2 tablespoons unsalted butter, melted

Preheat the oven to 350°F.

Stir together the cocoa powder, salt, sugar, cayenne, and garlic powder in a small bowl.

Combine the nuts, pumpkin seeds, and sesame seeds in a medium bowl and stir to mix. Drizzle the melted butter over and toss quickly to evenly coat the nuts. I like to use a rubber spatula for blending the nuts, to be sure the seasoning is well distributed. Sprinkle about half of the cocoa mixture over and toss well to mix. Repeat with the remaining cocoa mixture; applying in 2 batches helps assure the most even coating of the nuts.

Scatter the coated nuts on a rimmed baking sheet.

Bake until lightly toasted and aromatic, 15 to 20 minutes, gently stirring the nuts once or twice to ensure even toasting. Let cool on the baking sheet, then transfer to a serving bowl. If you are not serving within a few hours, store in an airtight container for up to 1 week.

Roasted Chickpeas *with Sumac*

I'm a card-carrying fan of chickpeas in all forms, from fresh roasted-in-the-shell to chickpea salads, braised chicken with chickpeas, you name it. So it's not too big a surprise that I find myself turning to chickpeas a few times in this book, including a couple in flour form (Chickpea Cake with Niçoise Olives and Shallots, page 137, and Onion Pakoras with Cilantro Sauce, page 139). Here the whole chickpeas are turned into a roasty snack. The quickest route is certainly using canned chickpeas (I prefer reduced-sodium). But you can start from dried chickpeas as well. Put 1 cup in a medium bowl and add enough cold water to cover by a generous couple of inches. Let sit at room temperature for 24 to 36 hours, then drain well and proceed as for the canned below.

Sumac is the fruit of a Middle Eastern bush, the dried berries sometimes available whole but often in ground form. A traditional garnish sprinkled over hummus among other common uses, sumac has a savory-lemony flavor that pairs well with chickpeas. Look for it in specialty spice markets or from online sources (see page 154). You can use paprika (smoked or sweet) instead.

| **Makes 6 to 8 servings**

---

2 (15.5-ounce) cans chickpeas, rinsed and well drained

2 tablespoons freshly squeezed lemon juice

2 tablespoons olive oil

2 teaspoons ground sumac

1 1/2 teaspoons kosher salt or flaky or coarse sea salt

Preheat the oven to 375°F. Line a rimmed baking sheet with parchment paper or a silicone baking mat.

Scatter the chickpeas on a double layer of paper towels and lay another sheet of paper towel on top, gently rolling the chickpeas between the towels with the palm of your hand to dry them.

Put the chickpeas in a medium bowl and add the lemon juice, olive oil, sumac, and salt. Toss well to evenly blend. Spread the chickpeas out in an even layer on the baking sheet. Bake until mostly crisp and lightly browned, about 1 hour, stirring the chickpeas every 15 minutes or so to ensure even toasting.

Let the chickpeas cool completely on the baking sheet (they'll crisp up a bit more) before transferring to a serving bowl, or to an airtight container for 1 to 2 days.

Moroccan Spiced Olives

Olives are a great salty snack in their natural form, but there are plenty of ways to jazz them up with various spices and seasonings. I often gravitate to the flavors of North Africa, which I do again here with cumin, coriander, lemon, and hot chiles. (The frequency with which cumin pops up in these pages echoes how often I reach for the jar at home; it's one of my favorite spices. I've always thought that if I ever opened a little restaurant I might dub it Cumin Get It.)

Not only are the olives delicious after they marinate, the oil is amazing, too. Consider using some of it as a dip for bread. Picholine is my top pick for type of green olive to use for this recipe. | **Makes 3 cups**

---

3 cups top-quality green olives (about 1 pound)

1 large lemon

1¼ cups olive oil

1 tablespoon coriander seeds

1 tablespoon cumin seeds

3 plump cloves garlic, thinly sliced

3 small whole dried hot chiles, broken in a few pieces, or 1 teaspoon red pepper flakes

Put the olives in a medium bowl. Use a vegetable peeler to remove the zest from the lemon in long strips. Add the lemon zest to the olives, then squeeze the juice from the lemon and pour that over the olives as well. Set aside.

Heat ¼ cup of the olive oil in a small skillet over medium-low heat. Add the coriander seeds and cumin seeds and cook, stirring often, until aromatic and just lightly browned, 2 to 3 minutes. Pour the spices and their oil over the olives. Add the remaining 1 cup olive oil, garlic, and chiles, stir gently to evenly mix all the ingredients, then cover the bowl and refrigerate for at least 1 day, and up to 7 days. Stir the olives a couple times each day.

About 1 hour before serving, take the olives from the refrigerator and transfer them to one large serving bowl or a few small serving bowls. Set out a small dish, too, for the olive pits.

Green Curry Crisp Tofu

To me, one of the greatest convenience ingredients to have on hand is a jar of Thai curry paste. I usually have one each of the red and green varieties in my refrigerator door, to have an easy way to add zip to sautéed vegetables for dinner, or to stir into a bowl of plain steamed rice for lunch. Here the highly flavored paste acts as something of an outside-in sauce, smeared inside a piece of tofu to add flavor without adding a mess-factor to this healthy snack. | **Makes 6 to 8 servings**

---

1 package (14 ounces) firm tofu

3 tablespoons finely minced green onion, white and pale green portions

1 teaspoon Thai green curry paste

1/2 teaspoon soy sauce, plus more for serving

2 tablespoons olive oil, plus more if needed

Drain the tofu and pat dry with paper towels. Cut the brick lengthwise into thirds, then cut each third crosswise into 6 even pieces, for 18 pieces total; they should be cubes about 1 1/2 inch by 3/4 inch and 1/2 inch thick. Use the tip of a small knife to cut a pocket in one long side of each piece of tofu, being careful not to cut through either of the other 3 sides.

In a small dish, stir together the green onion, curry paste, and soy sauce.

Use a small spoon (such as a demitasse spoon) or the tip of a small knife to spread about 1/2 teaspoon of the curry mixture in the pouch of each tofu piece. Pinch the piece of tofu from the sides to help open the pocket a bit, to make filling it easier.

Heat the olive oil in a large heavy skillet, preferably nonstick, over medium-high heat. When the pan is hot, add the tofu pieces and cook until browned and crisp, 3 to 4 minutes. Turn the pieces and brown well on the other side, 3 to 4 minutes longer. (You may find that a bit of extra oil is needed to help the second side crisp up well.)

Transfer the tofu to a platter or plate and serve warm, with a small dish of soy sauce alongside for dipping. The tofu will be best served right away.

Curry-Pickled Quail Eggs

Pickled eggs may not be among the most universal of bar snacks, but there certainly is a devoted audience of bar patrons who relish the vinegary nosh. Perhaps most popular among the British, it pops up in bars and pubs both trendy and dive-y around the globe.

There are a couple alternatives for serving these quail eggs. Rather than halved as I recommend here, you can keep the eggs whole and skewer each egg onto a small pick with a grape tomato for a flavorful cocktail bite. Or, in a less snacky context, quarter the eggs to serve as garnish for a simple green salad. | **Makes 6 to 8 servings**

---

1 cup cider vinegar or white wine vinegar
1 cup water
1/2 cup thinly sliced red onion
2 bay leaves, preferably fresh
1 tablespoon curry powder
8 allspice berries
6 whole cloves
2 teaspoons kosher salt or flaky or coarse sea salt
24 quail eggs

Combine the vinegar, water, onion, bay leaves, curry powder, allspice, cloves, and salt in a small saucepan and bring just to a boil over medium-high heat. Reduce the heat to medium-low and simmer for 5 minutes. Take the pan from the heat and let cool.

While the pickling liquid is cooling, put the quail eggs in a medium pan of cold water and bring just to a boil over medium-high heat.

Reduce the heat to medium and simmer for 3 minutes. Pour off the hot water and add cold water and plenty of ice to the pan to help cool the eggs quickly. When fully cooled, drain the eggs, peel them, and put them in a glass or ceramic bowl. Pour the cooled pickling mixture over, cover the bowl, and refrigerate for 24 to 48 hours.

Shortly before serving, remove the eggs from the pickling liquid, halve each one, and set them on a serving plate. Lift some of the red onion from the pickling liquid and finely chop about 2 tablespoons' worth. Top each of the egg halves with some of the pickled onion and serve.

Vegetables and Grains

On those occasions when you're being extra diligent about what you're eating and want to keep the indulgence factor down, you've got some great options in this chapter. Which further supports the idea that "snack food" can be a far cry from the junk food label it's often given— as the vegetable and grain-based recipes that follow can attest.

Oh, but don't worry. There's some indulgence in this chapter too! When that's your mood, the Crisp Avocado with Green Goddess Dip (page 134) and Deep-Fried Cornichons with Dill Sauce (page 140) are where you want to head.

Baby Artichokes *with Lemon-Chive Aioli*

The artichoke bar was raised for me on a trip to Rome when I tasted traditional *carciofi alla giudia*, or Jewish-style artichokes. The trimmed full-size artichoke is cooked whole, fried so that its leaves become potato-chip crisp and the heart remains tender. I was in heaven. In this recipe, baby artichoke pieces are roasted in a simplified homage to that classic. | **Makes 4 to 6 servings**

Lemon-Chive Aioli
- 1 large egg yolk
- 1 tablespoon freshly squeezed lemon juice
- 2 cloves garlic, finely minced or pressed
- 3/4 cup olive oil
- 1 teaspoon finely grated lemon zest
- Kosher salt or flaky or coarse sea salt
- Freshly ground white pepper
- 1 tablespoon finely chopped fresh chives

- 1 small lemon, halved
- 8 baby artichokes
- 2 tablespoons olive oil
- Kosher salt or flaky or coarse sea salt
- Freshly ground black pepper

To make the aioli, combine the egg yolk, juice, and garlic in a food processor and pulse to blend. With the blades running, add the oil a couple drops at a time until the mixture starts to thicken into an emulsion. Continue adding the rest of the oil in a thin, steady stream. Add the lemon zest with salt and white pepper to taste. Scrape down the sides and pulse a few more times to evenly mix. Transfer to a small serving bowl, stir in the chives, cover with plastic wrap, and refrigerate. The aioli will have a more balanced flavor if made at least 2 hours before serving; it can be made up to 2 days in advance.

Preheat the oven to 450°F. Fill a large bowl with water and squeeze in the juice from the lemon halves, adding the rinds to the water as well. Use your fingers to trim a couple of outer layers of leaves from one of the artichokes until you reach the tender, paler green/yellowish leaves toward the center. Trim the stem to about 2 inches and use a vegetable peeler or small knife to peel away the tough outer green skin from the base and stem. Cut the top down to about 2 inches from the base of the artichoke. Halve the artichoke and scrape out the choke (young artichokes may not have much). Cut each half into 3 or 4 wedges and put them in the lemon-water to avoid discoloration. Repeat.

Drain the artichokes and pat them dry on a towel or double-layer of paper towels. Rinse and dry the large bowl. Put the artichoke pieces in the bowl, drizzle the olive oil over, and add a good pinch of salt and pepper. Toss well, then arrange the slices on a rimmed baking sheet. Bake until the leaves are lightly browned and crisp and the base is tender, 12 to 15 minutes, turning the artichoke pieces halfway through. Transfer to a platter with the bowl of aioli alongside.

Fennel Bagna Cauda

Bagna cauda—or "hot bath" in Italian—is a simple dip of warm olive oil enhanced with garlic and anchovy. Typically served with a variety of vegetables for dipping, I opt here for the delightful crunch and light anise flavor of fresh fennel bulb to star. But certainly feel free to add radishes, cucumber slices, carrot sticks, cauliflower florets, or other favorite vegetables to the mix. You can use an extra-virgin olive oil if you like, though I prefer the milder flavor of a good virgin olive oil instead. | **Makes 4 to 6 servings**

---

2 large or 3 small fennel bulbs
1/2 cup olive oil
4 anchovy fillets, finely chopped
1 tablespoon finely minced or pressed garlic

Trim the stalks from the fennel at the points where they meet the bulb. Reserve the tender green fronds and discard the stalks (or save them for a batch of fish or vegetable stock). Cut away the tough base from each bulb and set each bulb upright on the cutting board. Halve the bulbs vertically, from the top toward the base. Cut out the tough core at the center, then separate the layers of fennel. Smaller tender pieces from the center can be served as is; other pieces should be cut into 1^{1}/2-inch-wide strips. Arrange the fennel pieces on a platter with a dipping bowl at the center.

Finely chop enough of the reserved fennel fronds to make 2 tablespoons; set aside. (Discard the rest, or save for another use.)

Warm the olive oil in a small saucepan over medium-low heat. When warm, stir in the anchovy and garlic. Cook gently, stirring occasionally, until the garlic and anchovies are aromatic, about 10 minutes. Take the pan from the heat and stir in the chopped fennel fronds. Pour the bagna cauda into the dipping bowl and serve while warm.

Quick-Pickled Vegetables

Feel free to play around with the combination of vegetables here; consider adding small whole button mushrooms, halved or quartered radishes, or jicama sticks to the mix. There's a small dose of spicy bite to these with the addition of red pepper flakes to the pickling liquids; you can temper the spice by cutting back on them. | **Makes 6 to 8 servings**

1 large English cucumber

3 medium carrots

12 ounces small cauliflower florets

2 sprigs fresh dill

2 cups distilled white vinegar

2 cups water

2 teaspoons kosher salt or flaky or coarse sea salt

2 teaspoons fennel seeds

2 teaspoons dill seeds

1 teaspoon brown mustard seeds

3/4 teaspoon red pepper flakes

Trim the ends from the cucumber and quarter it lengthwise. Use a small spoon to scoop out the seeds from center, then cut each portion across into 3 even pieces (roughly 4 inches long). Cut the carrots across into pieces about 4 inches long. Narrower ends of the carrots can be halved lengthwise, broader portions should be quartered.

Arrange the vegetables in layers in a medium heatproof bowl or dish just large enough to hold them, adding the dill sprigs at the midpoint.

Combine the vinegar, water, salt, fennel seeds, dill seeds, mustard seeds, and pepper flakes in a small saucepan. Bring just to a boil, then reduce the heat to medium-low and simmer for 1 minute. Carefully pour the hot pickling liquid over the vegetables and set aside to cool to room temperature. Cover the bowl and refrigerate for at least 2 hours, or up to 3 or 4 days. (The longer the vegetables hang out in the liquid, the more pickled—and spicy—the flavors will be.)

Lift the pickled vegetables from the liquid and arrange them in a bowl or on a plate, brushing off any bits of the seasonings that may be clinging to them.

Tempura Green Beans *with Tapenade Dip*

For a shortcut, you can purchase tapenade to use for the dip—if the one you're using is chunky, give it a brief whirl in a food processor for a more dip-friendly consistency. For homemade, briny-salty kalamata olives are a good choice; dry-cured olives can be a bit bitter for this use, and Niçoise, while delicious, are a bit persnickety to pit. Don't bother with canned black olives for this recipe. Going with rice flour makes this gluten-free. | **Makes 6 servings**

Tapenade Dip

- 1 cup pitted black olives (about 6 ounces)
- 2 tablespoons capers
- 1 anchovy fillet, chopped
- 1 teaspoon finely minced or pressed garlic
- 1/4 cup freshly squeezed lemon juice, plus more if needed
- 2 tablespoons olive oil

Tempura Batter

- 1 large egg
- 1 cup ice water, plus more if needed
- 1 cup sweet (white) rice flour or all-purpose flour

- Vegetable oil, for frying
- 1 pound green beans, trimmed, rinsed, and well dried

To make the dip, combine the olives, capers, anchovy, and garlic in a food processor and pulse until finely chopped and well blended, scraping down the sides as needed. Add the lemon juice and olive oil and pulse a few times to blend. If the texture is too chunky or thick for a dip, puree it well and add a bit more lemon juice or water if needed. Transfer to a small serving bowl. It can be made up to 2 days ahead, covered, and refrigerated. Let it come to room temperature before serving.

Pour about 2 inches of oil into a large heavy saucepan (the oil should not come more than halfway up the sides of the pan). Bring to 375°F over medium heat. When the oil is nearly to temperature, make the batter. Beat the egg with a fork in a bowl, then beat in the ice water. Add the flour gradually, beating gently as you go; avoid overmixing or the batter will become heavy. It should be of thin enough consistency to just delicately coat the beans. If it's a bit too thick, beat in another tablespoon or two of ice water.

Drop a small handful of green beans into the batter and stir to coat. Lift them out one by one with a fork or tongs, allowing excess batter to drip off, then gently add them individually to the hot oil to avoid clumping. Fry until crisp and lightly browned, 2 to 3 minutes. Scoop them out with a slotted spoon and drain on paper towels. Continue to coat and fry in batches, allowing the oil to reheat between batches as needed. Stir the batter gently between batches as well, especially if using rice flour, which quickly begins to settle.

Stir the dip to remix and set it in the center of a platter, surrounded by the tempura green beans. Serve right away.

Crisp Avocado *with Green Goddess Dip*

A fan of avocado in all forms, I'll admit that this treatment is a bit more decadent than some. A light coating of tarragon-flecked bread crumbs creates a crunchy contrast to the creamy texture of the avocado slices. | **Makes 4 to 6 servings**

Green Goddess Dip

- 1/2 cup top-quality mayonnaise
- 1/4 cup buttermilk
- 2 tablespoons tarragon vinegar or white wine vinegar
- 2 tablespoons minced shallot or onion
- 2 tablespoons chopped fresh flat-leaf parsley
- 1 tablespoon chopped fresh tarragon
- 1 tablespoon chopped fresh chives
- 3 anchovy fillets, chopped

- 2 large ripe but firm avocados
- 1 large egg
- 1/2 cup buttermilk
- 1 teaspoon kosher salt or flaky or coarse sea salt
- 1 1/2 cups panko bread crumbs
- 2 tablespoons minced fresh tarragon
- Vegetable oil, for frying

To make the dip, combine the mayonnaise, buttermilk, vinegar, shallot, parsley, tarragon, chives, and anchovies in a mini food processor or blender and blend until smooth. Transfer the dip to a small serving bowl. Cover and refrigerate until needed. The flavors will be best if the dip is made at least 1 hour in advance; it can be made up to 1 day ahead.

Halve and pit the avocados, then peel away the skin and cut each half into 1/2-inch-thick slices. You should have 20 to 24 slices.

Beat the egg well in a shallow bowl, then beat in the buttermilk and salt. Let sit for a few minutes so the salt has a chance to dissolve, then beat again to mix. Combine the panko bread crumbs and tarragon on a plate and use your fingers to evenly combine. Dip a few avocado slices in the egg mixture, then lift them out and allow the excess to drip off. Coat the slices well with the bread crumbs, pressing gently to help the crumbs adhere, then patting to remove excess. Set the coated slices aside on a plate and continue coating the remaining avocado slices.

Heat about 1/4 inch of the oil in a large skillet over medium heat. Working in batches, cook the coated avocado slices in the oil just until nicely browned, about 2 minutes per side. Set aside on paper towels to drain while frying the remaining avocado slices.

Put the dip in the center of a plate or platter, arrange the crisp avocado slices around, and serve right away.

Wasabi Pea *and* Rice Squares

This snack is inspired by that crusty rice goodness that lines a paella pan after cooking, and the Persian dish of *tadig* that's beloved for the rich, crisp layer of rice that forms on the bottom of the pan. I depart from either Spanish or Persian flavor influences here, however, opting instead to flavor the rice with a bit of zing from wasabi peas. If you're a big fan of wasabi, you can add 1 tablespoon of prepared wasabi with the finely crushed peas. The wasabi peas—which are available at Asian markets and with other Asian ingredients in well-stocked grocery stores—should be finely crushed so they'll mix most evenly with the rice. I like to pulse them in the food processor for best results. | **Makes 8 servings**

---

2 cups water

1½ teaspoons kosher salt or flaky or coarse
   sea salt

1 cup basmati rice

1 cup ground or very finely crushed
   wasabi peas

3 to 4 tablespoons vegetable oil

Combine the water and 1 teaspoon of the salt in a small saucepan and bring to a boil over medium-high heat. Stir in the rice, cover the pan, and cook over low heat until the rice is tender and all the water has been absorbed, about 18 minutes.

Transfer the rice to a medium bowl, add the wasabi peas and remaining ½ teaspoon of salt. Stir quickly with a fork until the peas are evenly blended with the rice. Turn the hot rice mixture into a lightly oiled 8- or 9-inch square cake pan and spread out with the back of the fork to form an even layer. Press down with your lightly oiled fingers to compress the rice in a compact layer. (Wait a couple of minutes if

the rice is too hot to touch, but it's best to form the rice while warm.)

Let the rice cool to room temperature, then cover the pan with plastic wrap and refrigerate until well chilled and firm, about 4 hours.

Heat 2 tablespoons of the vegetable oil in a large, heavy skillet over medium heat. While the oil is heating, turn the rice out onto a cutting board and cut it into 16 squares. Add half of the squares to the skillet and cook until lightly browned and crisp, 4 to 5 minutes. Carefully turn the squares and brown on the second side, about 4 minutes longer, adding a bit more oil to the pan if needed. (If the skillet gets dry, the rice won't become as crisp as it should.) Transfer the crisped squares to a serving plate, heat 1 tablespoon of the remaining oil in the skillet, and brown the remaining squares. These will be at their best served shortly after browning, while warm.

Pan-Fried Chiles *with Sesame Seed Salt*

The simplicity of this recipe is enticing. No more than 15 minutes from start to finish and you've got an addictive snack, the whole chiles even sporting their own perfect handle—the stem. The trick is to get your hands on the chiles that work best for this type of preparation: small chiles with thin skins and a flavor that isn't crazy hot. Padróns from Spain and shishito chiles from Japan are two top contenders. Both are in season primarily during the summer, when you may find them at a local farmers' market or from specialty purveyors, though some suppliers may have them available more often. There are online resources as well (see page 153).

While most of the time, padrón and shishito chiles are on the mild-to-moderate side of the Scoville scale, now and then you'll find a pepper that's got some heat to it. I've heard it referred to as something of a gastro version of Russian roulette. Just so you're warned.

| **Makes 4 to 6 servings**

---

1 tablespoon white sesame seeds

1 teaspoon kosher salt or flaky or coarse sea salt

1 pound whole padrón or shishito chiles, stems intact, rinsed and dried

1 tablespoon olive oil

Put the sesame seeds in a small skillet over medium heat and toast until they are just lightly browned, stirring or gently tossing the seeds often, 2 to 3 minutes. Transfer the seeds to a small bowl or plate and set aside to cool (leaving them in the hot pan risks burning).

If you have a spice grinder (see page 10), pulse the cooled sesame seeds a few times to finely chop them. Or you can crush the sesame seeds in a mortar and pestle. Transfer the seeds to a small dish and stir in the salt.

Put the chiles in a large bowl, drizzle the olive oil over, and toss well to evenly coat.

Heat a large skillet over medium-high heat. When the pan is good and hot, add half of the chiles and cook, gently tossing or stirring the chiles often, until lightly charred, 3 to 4 minutes. The chiles should be just about tender but still holding their shape. Transfer the chiles to a large serving bowl and set aside while pan-frying the remaining chiles in the same fashion.

With all the chiles in the bowl, scatter the sesame salt over and toss for a moment or two to evenly mix. Serve right away.

Chickpea Cake *with Niçoise Olives and Shallots*

Tiny little Niçoise olives are ideal here; they have delightful flavor but are hard to pit—so they're used whole. Be sure to give your guests the heads-up that the pits are intact before they dig in. You can use other flavorful types of black olive if you like. Larger olives should be pitted and coarsely chopped before scattering over the chickpea batter. I love the flavor of sage with this recipe as well; you can stir 1 tablespoon finely slivered fresh sage into the batter with the shallots. Look for chickpea flour with specialty baking goods in well-stocked grocery stores, in natural food stores, or online (see page 153). | **Makes 6 to 8 servings**

---

1 cup chickpea flour

1 teaspoon kosher salt or flaky or coarse sea salt

1/4 teaspoon freshly ground black pepper

1 cup water

3 to 4 tablespoons olive oil

1 cup thinly sliced shallots

1/2 cup Niçoise olives, drained

Use a whisk to stir together the chickpea flour, salt, and pepper in a medium bowl. Whisk in the water and 2 tablespoons of the olive oil, forming a smooth batter that should have the consistency of heavy cream. Set aside.

Preheat the broiler. Set an oven rack 4 to 5 inches below the heating element.

Heat 1 tablespoon of the olive oil in a large heavy skillet, preferably cast iron, over medium heat. Add the shallots and cook, stirring occasionally, until tender but not browned, 4 to 5 minutes. Set aside to cool for 10 to 15 minutes.

Stir the shallots into the chickpea batter. Return the skillet to medium heat. Add a bit more olive oil to the skillet if needed so there's a thin sheen across the bottom. Use a ladle to spoon half of the chickpea batter into the hot pan, spreading it out evenly. Scatter half of the olives over and cook until the surface is no longer shiny and the edges are lightly browned, 3 to 4 minutes. With the help of a metal spatula, slide the chickpea cake onto one side of a rimmed baking sheet. Repeat with the remaining batter, setting the second cake on the baking sheet alongside the first. Broil until the chickpea cakes are lightly browned on top, about 2 minutes.

Let the cakes cool to room temperature, then cut them into wedges and arrange on a plate or small platter to serve. These will be best served shortly after cooking.

Onion Pakoras *with Cilantro Sauce*

For you onion ring lovers out there, I offer something a bit different with this India-inspired version of fried onions. I'm a big fan of chickpea flour; its savory, nutty flavor pairs beautifully with onions. An added bonus is that chickpea flour is gluten-free. A mandoline or other handy slicer (see page 10) is ideal for the onions here; the slices should be just thin enough to be flexible so they form tidy little clusters when blended with the batter, but they don't need to be paper thin. Look for chickpea flour with specialty baking goods in well-stocked grocery stores, in natural food stores, or online (see page 153). | **Makes 6 servings**

Cilantro Sauce

- 1 cup moderately packed cilantro leaves
- 3 tablespoons red wine vinegar
- 3 tablespoons olive oil
- 1 teaspoon minced jalapeño
- 1/2 teaspoon ground coriander
- 1/4 teaspoon kosher salt or flaky or coarse sea salt

- 3/4 cup chickpea flour
- 2 tablespoons finely minced cilantro
- 1 teaspoon ground cumin
- 3/4 teaspoon kosher salt or flaky or coarse sea salt
- 1/2 teaspoon baking soda
- 1/2 cup cold water
- Vegetable oil, for frying
- 1 medium yellow onion, quartered and very thinly sliced

To make the sauce, combine the cilantro, vinegar, olive oil, jalapeño, coriander, and salt in a mini food processor or blender and process until smooth, scraping down the sides as needed. Transfer to a small serving bowl and set aside.

(The sauce can be made up to 1 day in advance and refrigerated, covered.)

Use a whisk to stir together the chickpea flour, cilantro, cumin, salt, and baking soda in a medium bowl. Whisk in the water to form a smooth batter. Set aside for 10 minutes.

While the batter is sitting, pour about 2 inches of oil into a large heavy saucepan (the oil should not come more than halfway up the sides of the pan). Bring to 365°F over medium heat.

Use a wooden spoon to stir the batter, then add the onion, stirring well to evenly blend. Scoop up a heaping tablespoon of the onion mixture and gently add it to the hot oil. Repeat to form 4 or 5 more *pakoras* and fry until nicely browned and crisp, 3 to 4 minutes, gently turning the *pakoras* once or twice for even cooking. If they brown too quickly, the inside risks not being cooked through; reduce the oil temperature a bit if needed. Lift out the *pakoras* with a slotted spoon and set aside on paper towels to drain while frying the remaining batter.

Arrange the *pakoras* on a plate or platter with the sauce alongside for dipping.

Deep-Fried Cornichons *with Dill Sauce*

It wasn't all that long ago that I had my first fried pickle, a treat from the South where slices of snack dills are often used. I gave the idea a touch of a French accent by using little cornichons instead. Feel free to omit the sour cream from the sauce recipe and use just yogurt instead; the results will be tangier, but a bit lighter. | **Makes 4 to 6 servings**

Dill Sauce
- ¹/₂ cup plain yogurt (preferably whole or low-fat)
- ¹/₂ cup sour cream
- 2 tablespoons minced fresh dill
- ¹/₂ teaspoon finely minced or pressed garlic
- ¹/₂ teaspoon kosher salt or flaky or coarse sea salt

- Vegetable oil, for frying
- 2 cups cornichons (about 12 ounces)
- ¹/₂ cup all-purpose flour
- 1 large egg
- ¹/₄ cup buttermilk or whole milk
- Pinch of kosher salt or flaky or coarse sea salt
- 1¹/₂ cups plain dried bread crumbs
- ¹/₂ teaspoon cayenne pepper

To make the sauce, stir together the yogurt, sour cream, dill, garlic, and salt in a small serving bowl. Refrigerate until you are ready to serve. The flavor will be best if made at least 1 hour in advance; the sauce can be made up to 1 day ahead.

Pour about 2 inches of oil into a large heavy saucepan (the oil should not come more than halfway up the sides of the pan). Bring to 375°F over medium heat.

While the oil is heating, scatter the cornichons on paper towels and pat dry. Put the flour in a medium bowl. Beat together the egg, buttermilk, and salt in a shallow bowl. Toss together the bread crumbs and cayenne in another medium bowl.

Add the cornichons to the flour and toss well to evenly coat. Lift out a handful of the cornichons, tossing them well in your hands to remove excess flour, and add them to the beaten egg. Use a fork to gently turn the cornichons to evenly coat with the egg mixture. Lift out a cornichon or two at a time, allowing excess egg to drip off, then add them to the bread crumbs. Use a clean fork to toss the cornichons in the crumbs to evenly coat. Lift out the cornichons, shaking gently to remove excess crumbs, and set aside on a large plate while coating the remaining cornichons.

Gently add 10 or so of the coated cornichons to the hot oil and fry until nicely browned and crisp, 2 to 3 minutes. Lift out the cornichons with a slotted spoon and drain on paper towels. Continue frying the cornichons in batches, allowing the oil to reheat as needed between batches.

Set the bowl of sauce in the center of a serving plate and arrange the fried cornichons around. Serve right away, though they're still delicious at room temperature as well.

Puffed Rice Squares *with Curry and Coconut*

Think of these as a fully grown-up version of those Rice Krispie Treats we loved so much as kids (and may still do as adults!). I prefer the texture and character of traditional puffed rice cereal, but other puffed cereals can be good, too, such as puffed kamut or puffed wheat. Having no nostalgic attachment to marshmallows, I tried alternative means to hold these treats together. But ultimately, it's the marshmallows that do the trick. | **Makes 12 servings**

3/4 cup flaked coconut

3/4 cup unsalted hulled (green) pumpkin seeds

4 cups plain puffed rice cereal

1/4 cup unsalted butter

2 teaspoons curry powder

1 teaspoon kosher salt or flaky or coarse sea salt

24 large marshmallows

Preheat the oven to 350°F. Generously butter an 8- or 9-inch square cake pan.

Scatter the coconut in one small baking dish and the pumpkin seeds in another. Toast both in the oven until lightly browned and nutty smelling: 5 to 7 minutes for the pumpkin seeds and 8 to 10 minutes for the coconut, stirring each once or twice to ensure even toasting. Set aside to cool.

Combine the puffed rice, coconut, and pumpkin seeds in a large bowl and toss to mix. Melt the butter in a saucepan over medium heat. Stir in the curry powder and salt and cook until aromatic, stirring, about 1 minute. Add the marshmallows and cook, stirring gently, until melted and well blended, 3 to 5 minutes. Drizzle the curry mixture over the puffed rice and quickly toss to evenly coat. Transfer to the prepared pan, pressing down with the back of the spoon to form an even layer. Set aside until cooled and set, about 1 hour. Cut into squares, transfer to a platter, and serve. If not serving right away, store in an airtight container for up to 1 day.

STIRRING NOTES

When you're told to stir something now and then while it's taking a spin in the oven, it's always best to take the pan from the oven, set it on a heatproof surface, and close the oven door right away. Stir as needed, then pop it back in the oven. This helps keep the oven temperature consistent. If you hold the door open while you do the stirring, it's likely you lose enough heat that the oven will kick into reheat mode when you close the door. That blast of heat may be enough to burn the food, especially small, delicate items such as the shredded coconut and seeds here. They can go from "just right" to bitter in the blink of an eye.

Dips and Spreads

There are a number of dips and spreads that are partnered with
specific recipes throughout the book; see the box on page 150
for a listing. In the pages that follow are some additional versatile
dips and spreads that you may want to turn to now and then
to accompany a variety of the crackers, breads, chips, and other recipes
in the book. If you're rushed for time or planning a low-maintenance
party, you can also pair these dips and spreads with store-bought pita
bread, baguette slices, chips, crackers, or a crudités platter.
Your homemade dip as a centerpiece can be a great starting point
for the simplest of snack-time offerings.

Cucumber *and* **Radish Tzatziki**

Tzatziki has been one of my favorite dips for ages now; a bowl of tzatziki and some pita bread makes a delightful lunch in my book. Here, the classic yogurt-cucumber combo gains a bit of peppery crunch with the addition of radish. I use the large holes on a standard box grater to grate the vegetables for this dip, so quick and easy. This is ideal as a dip for the Cumin Lentil Crackers on page 74 or an herb variation of the pita chips on page 33. I also love to spoon it over sliced tomatoes for a simple salad, and I sometimes top off lamb burgers with a dollop or two.
| **Makes about 2¹/₂ cups**

1¹/₂ cups plain yogurt (preferably whole or low-fat)

1 cup grated English cucumber

¹/₂ cup grated radish

2 tablespoons minced fresh cilantro or flat-leaf parsley

¹/₂ teaspoon finely minced or pressed garlic

¹/₂ teaspoon kosher salt or flaky or coarse sea salt

Stir together the yogurt, cucumber, radish, cilantro, garlic, and salt in a medium bowl. Transfer the dip to a small serving bowl. If not serving right away (the flavors will be best if made at least 1 hour in advance), cover and refrigerate until needed. The dip can be made up to 2 days in advance.

Black Bean Dip

Nothing could be much easier than this dip—just toss everything in the food processor and give it a whirl. Think of it as something of a southwestern twist on hummus, delicious with pita chips or corn chips, or as a cohort to the Spicy Tortilla Crisps with Queso Fundido on page 34.
| **Makes 1¹/₂ cups**

---

1 (15-ounce) can black beans, rinsed and well drained

¹/₄ cup finely chopped onion

¹/₄ cup finely chopped fresh cilantro or flat-leaf parsley

1 teaspoon finely grated lime zest

3 tablespoons freshly squeezed lime juice

1 tablespoon olive oil

¹/₂ teaspoon ground cumin

¹/₄ teaspoon kosher salt or flaky or coarse **sea salt**

Tabasco sauce

Combine the black beans, onion, cilantro, lime zest, lime juice, olive oil, cumin, salt, and a few dashes of Tabasco sauce in a food processor. Pulse until smooth and well blended, scraping down the sides as needed. Transfer the dip to a small serving bowl. If not serving right away (the flavors will be best if made at least 1 hour in advance), cover and refrigerate until needed. Allow the dip to come to room temperature before serving. The dip can be made up to 2 days in advance.

Roasted Pepper *and* Walnut Spread

This is a lush spread that hints at Middle Eastern flavors with roasted red peppers blended with toasted walnuts. It's a delicious option to adorn many types of cracker from a simple The Best Crackers (page 64) to bolder Rye Crackers with Caraway (page 76). Harissa is a favorite condiment that's most always in my refrigerator. It is common to North Africa and made in a number of forms. My favorite type includes both hot chiles and roasted bell pepper, olive oil, and spices. Traditionally served alongside couscous, it's a tasty way to add bright flavor to any number of dishes. Harissas can vary quite a lot in heat level, so adjust the amount used accordingly. Sriracha tends to be quite a lot hotter, but a small dab of it can be used instead. | **Makes about 1¼ cups**

1 clove garlic, crushed

1¼ cups toasted walnuts

1 red bell pepper, roasted and chopped (see page 14)

2 tablespoons olive oil

1 tablespoon red wine vinegar, plus more as needed

1 teaspoon harissa or other chile paste or sauce, plus more as needed

½ teaspoon kosher salt or flaky or coarse sea salt, plus more as needed

Put the garlic in a food processor and pulse until finely chopped. Scrape down the sides of the bowl and add the walnuts, pulsing until they are finely chopped. Add the bell pepper, olive oil, vinegar, harissa, and salt and process until well blended and smooth. Taste the spread for seasoning, adding more vinegar, harissa, or salt to taste.

Transfer the spread to a small serving bowl. If you are not serving right away, cover and refrigerate. The spread can be made up to 3 days in advance; let it come to room temperature before serving.

Feta-Lemon Spread

This spread has bright flavors from the briny cheese and tart lemon, a great complement to pita chips or as a topping for slices of the Olive Focaccia with Lemon on page 52. The combination of ingredients will make a great dip, too, for vegetables or bread sticks if you increase the yogurt to $1/2$ cup and thin the mixture with a bit more lemon juice. | **Makes about $1^1/4$ cups**

---

6 ounces feta cheese

$1/4$ cup plain yogurt (preferably whole or low-fat)

1 teaspoon finely grated lemon zest

1 tablespoon freshly squeezed lemon juice

$1/2$ teaspoon minced fresh oregano, or 1 teaspoon minced fresh flat-leaf parsley

Kosher salt or flaky or coarse sea salt

Freshly ground white pepper

Grate the feta into a medium bowl using the large holes of a box grater. Stir in the yogurt, lemon zest, lemon juice, and oregano. Stir well to mix, then season to taste with salt and white pepper. Transfer the spread to a small serving bowl. If not serving right away (the flavors will be best if made at least 1 hour in advance), cover and refrigerate until needed. The dip can be made up to 2 days in advance.

Miso-Spinach Dip

Miso is a Japanese fermented soybean paste that is often used in soups, dressings, and marinades. There are a range of types of miso paste. The white used here is among the milder and more versatile in flavor; others move up the scale of intensity. This is a great dip for the Kabocha Squash Chips on page 21, the Soy-Wasabi Wonton Crisps on page 32, or the next veggie tray that you make up for a party. | **Makes about 3/4 cup**

---

1 teaspoon olive oil

1 teaspoon toasted sesame oil

1/2 cup finely chopped onion

6 cups moderately packed baby spinach (about 6 ounces), rinsed and well dried

3 tablespoons sake, dry white wine, or water

1 tablespoon white miso

Heat the olive oil and sesame oil in a medium skillet over medium heat. Add the onion and cook, stirring, until tender and aromatic, 3 to 4 minutes. Add the spinach, a handful at a time, stirring until each addition is fully wilted before adding the next, about 5 minutes total. When all of the spinach has been added, stir in the sake and miso. Reduce the heat to medium-low and cook gently until the spinach is very tender and the mixture is well blended, 2 to 3 minutes.

Set the spinach aside to cool. Transfer to a food processor and pulse until smooth. If the dip is quite thick, drizzle in a teaspoon or two of water and pulse to blend.

Transfer the dip to a small serving bowl. If not serving right away, cover and refrigerate until needed. Allow the dip to come to room temperature before serving. The dip can be made up to 2 days in advance.

Artichoke–Roasted Garlic Spread

Much as I love that classic cheesy hot artichoke dip that's a staple of appetizer lists and bar snack menus, I find it a bit rich for frequent indulgence. This version of artichoke dip is much lighter, mixed with a puree of roasted garlic rather than mayonnaise. For an even quicker version, you may find roasted garlic available in the deli section of well-stocked grocery stores. Slices of baguette or tortilla chips are ideal to serve with this spread, or whip up the herb variation of the Pita Chips with Hazelnut and Parmesan on page 33. If you've got a toaster oven, certainly feel free to use that for roasting the garlic. | **Makes about 1¹/₄ cups**

---

1 large head garlic
1 (14-ounce) can quartered artichoke hearts, rinsed and well drained
2 tablespoons olive oil
2 tablespoons freshly squeezed lemon juice
Kosher salt or flaky or coarse sea salt
Freshly ground black pepper

Preheat the oven to 375°F.

Remove the papery outer skin from the garlic and set the head on a piece of aluminum foil. Wrap the foil up around the garlic to fully enclose it and bake until the garlic is quite tender when squeezed, about 40 minutes. Set aside to cool.

Separate the cloves from the head and squeeze the tender garlic from each. Put the garlic in a food processor and pulse until very finely chopped, scraping down the sides as needed. Add the artichoke hearts, olive oil, and lemon juice and pulse until the artichoke hearts are finely chopped and well blended with the garlic, scraping down the sides once or twice. The mixture should retain a bit of a chunky texture but be fine enough to easily spread onto a cracker. Taste the mixture for seasoning, adding salt and pepper to taste, pulsing to blend in the seasonings.

Transfer the spread to a serving bowl and serve. If not serving right away (the flavors will be best if made at least 1 hour in advance), cover and refrigerate until needed. Allow the dip to come to room temperature before serving. The dip can be made up to 3 days in advance.

Deviled Ham *with Pickled Peppers*

I ask at the deli counter for them to cut me a piece of ham (I like Black Forest ham) about ¹/₂ inch thick for this use, then at home I dice the ham before mincing it in the food processor. If the only ham you're able to get is thinly sliced, it will work fine, too; the resulting spread may just have a finer texture. Any type of pickled pepper can be used here, from sport peppers to pickled jalapeños. Different pickled pepper varieties vary in heat level, so you may want to adjust the amount according to your taste and the type of pepper chosen. This will be particularly tasty with the Rosemary Cornmeal Crackers on page 70, but it really works well with most any cracker. Or just a slice of baguette for that matter! | **Makes about 1¹/₄ cups**

8 ounces thick-cut ham, diced

2 tablespoons chopped pickled peppers

2 tablespoons top-quality mayonnaise, plus more if needed

1 teaspoon sherry vinegar, plus more as needed

1 teaspoon Dijon mustard, plus more as needed

Combine the ham and pickled peppers in a food processor and pulse until they are finely chopped and well blended, scraping down the sides as needed. Avoid overprocessing; the mixture should have a bit of a coarse texture, not become a smooth puree.

Add the mayonnaise, vinegar, and mustard to the processor and pulse three or four times to blend. Taste the mixture for seasoning, adding a bit more vinegar or mustard to taste. If the mixture is a bit dry, add another tablespoon or so of mayonnaise for a more spreadable texture.

Transfer the deviled ham to a serving bowl. If you are not serving right away, cover and refrigerate until you are ready to serve. The flavor will be best if made at least 2 hours in advance, but it can be prepared up to 3 days ahead. Allow the spread to come to room temperature before serving.

OTHER DIPS AND SAUCES

Tapenade Dip (page 132)

Lemon-Chive Aioli (page 129)

Dill Sauce (page 140)

Horseradish Sauce (page 97)

Cilantro Sauce (page 139)

Grainy Mustard Dip (page 104)

Herbed Clam Dip (page 18)

Shopping Resources

Here are some online or specialty resources I've used to source products needed in these recipes. Consider them as options should you have trouble finding some of these ingredients at stores or markets in your area. Resources listed without an address have no brick-and-mortar retail outlet of their own.

Bob's Red Mill
5000 Southeast International Way
Milwaukie, Oregon 97222
(800) 349-2173
www.bobsredmill.com
Many types of flours, meals, starches, grains, and other baking items, with special attention given to gluten-free selections. Among products for these recipes you'll find sorghum flour, chickpea flour, and sweet (white) and brown rice flours. There is a brick-and-mortar store near Portland, Oregon, distribution through retail channels, and online sales.

Chukar Cherries
320 Wine Country Road
Prosser, Washington 99350-0510
(800) 624-9544
www.chukar.com
Dried cherries and berries produced without additives or preservatives. This is an ideal source for the Toasted Walnuts with Tart Cherries and Rosemary recipe on page 110. There are brick-and-mortar stores at their company headquarters in Prosser (eastern Washington) and at Seattle's Pike Place Market, plus online sales.

Melissa's Produce
(800) 588-0151
www.melissas.com
All types of fresh produce, from the everyday apple to the exotic lychee. They have padrón and shishito chiles available in season, which I use for the Pan-Fried Chiles with Sesame Seed Salt (page 136). They offer online sales and distribution through retail channels.

Nuts.com
(800) 558-6887
http://nuts.com
This website offers a huge range of pantry items, from nuts and dried fruits to grains and dried beans. I found unsweetened coconut chips here for the Coconut Crisps with Basil and Chiles (page 28). Primarily online sales.

SaltWorks
16240 Woodinville-Redmond Road NE
Woodinville, Washington 98072
(800) 353-7258
www.seasalt.com
A vast array of salts from around the world, including French fleur de sel, smoked salts, English Maldon salt, and many other types of gourmet pure sea salts. Primarily online sales, though there is a small retail shop in their warehouse north of Seattle.

Theo Chocolate
3400 Phinney Avenue North
Seattle, Washington 98103
(206) 632-5100
www.theochocolate.com
A small, organic bean-to-bar chocolate factory in Seattle. They sell tins of cocoa nibs, which I call for in the Dark Chocolate Oat Cookies (page 87). They have a brick-and-mortar store at their Seattle factory, plus online sales.

World Spice Merchants
1509 Western Avenue
Seattle, Washington 98101
(206) 682-7274
www.worldspice.com
Wide range of spices (including sumac and Aleppo pepper), dried chiles, dried herbs, spice blends, as well as teas. They offer online sales, plus there is a brick-and-mortar store in Seattle near Pike Place Market.

About the Author

Cynthia Nims is a lifelong Northwesterner who reveled in growing up surrounded by great food—both in her mother's kitchen and exploring the region with her family. After graduating from the University of Puget Sound (Tacoma, Washington) with a Bachelor of Science degree in mathematics and a second major in French literature, Cynthia followed her dreams and went to France to study cooking at La Varenne Ecole de Cuisine. There, she received the Grand Diplôme d'Etudes Culinaires and worked on numerous cookbooks with the school's president, Anne Willan.

The author of more than a dozen cookbooks, Cynthia's most recent book is *Gourmet Game Night*. She also wrote four titles in the Northwest Homegrown Cookbook Series, and coauthored *Rover's: Recipes from Seattle's Chef in the Hat* with chef Thierry Rautureau. Cynthia also contributed content on Northwest cuisine to Williams-Sonoma's *Savoring America,* and to *Culinaria: The United States.*

Previously editor of *Simply Seafood* magazine and food editor of *Seattle* magazine, Cynthia now is a freelance contributor to *Seattle, Cooking Light, Alaska Airlines Magazine,* and other magazines. She is an active member of the International Association of Culinary Professionals (having recently served as the president of the board of directors) and Les Dames d'Escoffier. Cynthia and her husband enjoy homemade salty snacks in the comfort of their Seattle home. For more information, visit www.cynthianims.com.

Index

Library of Congress Cataloging-in-Publication Data

Nims, Cynthia C.
  Salty snacks : make your own chips, crisps, crackers, pretzels, dips,
and other savory bites / Cynthia Nims. — 1st ed.
       p. cm.
  Summary: "This collection of more than 75 recipes for savory chips,
crisps, crackers, pretzels, breads, nuts, and more puts a fresh, crunchy
spin on homemade snacks"— Provided by publisher.
  Includes index.
1. Snack foods. I. Title.
  TX740.N564 2012
  641.5'3—dc23

                              2012008152

ISBN 978-1-60774-181-7
eISBN 978-1-60774-182-4

Printed in China

Design by Colleen Cain

10 9 8 7 6 5 4 3 2 1

First Edition